FOREWORD

THIS gift-book is the story of the First Citizen and head of our Empire, written more particularly for his younger fellow-citizens, the schoolboys and schoolgirls of Great and Greater Britain, who are growing up to take their places in the Commonwealth of nations.

It is to help them perhaps to fill those places a little better by understanding what such citizenship means; and it is to commemorate the Coronation, the ceremony when the King-Emperor is consecrated to the service of his country and people at the place, and by the beautiful old rites, which have been used in the crowning of our monarchs for about a thousand years.

King George has already spent many years of his life in that service, especially devoting himself to the youth of the Empire. As he said in Australia: "Take care of the children and the country will take care of itself."

That has always been his aim and ideal, to care for the younger generation. During the years after the Great War, as Duke of York, he and the Duchess visited many parts of the Empire, and he thus became known personally to thousands and thousands of those who now call him King and who can think of him *not* merely as someone pictured on a coin or stamp, but as a friend, particularly of all boys and girls.

During his world tour, King George realised the meaning of those letters to be found on every penny we handle: "BRITT: OMN: REX . . . IND: IMP."—King of All the Britains . . . Emperor of India. "All the Britains"—all the British Dominions beyond the seas, stretching round the globe circlewise, like the Imperial Crown itself, set with great jewels like Canada, Australia, India, New Zealand, South Africa and with lesser gems, though no less bright, like Ceylon, the West Indies, Rhodesia, Newfoundland, Malta and Gibraltar. It proves how much meaning can be packed into just those seventeen letters on a copper coin.

He made a speech at Canberra in Australia which his subjects of the Dominions will not easily forget: "The present day marks the end of one epoch and the beginning of another, and one's thoughts turn instinctively to what the future may have in store especially for the new generation. One's own life would hardly be worth living without its dreams of better things, and the life of a nation without such dreams of a better and larger future would be poor indeed."

These words and their full meaning make a fine Coronation lesson for all boys and girls who are citizens of the Empire.

Just think for a moment how wonderful it would be if, to celebrate the great day, there could be a huge assembly of school-children from all the different Dominions, Colonies and States, large and small: what a sight it would be with all the different dresses, faces and languages— yet all using English as a common tongue.

How much they could tell each other of their own countries and customs. Indian children would speak of palms and palaces, temples and jungle creatures; Australian boys and girls could describe the Bush, sheep-farms, rivers lost in the sands of huge plains; South Africa, the veldt with its wonderful flowers and sunsets, Table Bay and the Cape where two oceans meet; the Canadian children would speak of great cities, great rivers, great lakes, pine forests and snow in the Rockies, and their school camps with swimming, rowing, riding, whilst from the West Indies would come stories of earthquakes, coral strands and hurricanes.

All would bring to the gathering something different belonging to their particular part of the Empire, and when all these pieces were fitted together, it would make a whole, finer and more beautiful than the separate bits, big or small. For that is the best meaning of Empire, that is the heritage which belongs to all British boys and girls and of which they cannot possibly be too proud—the wonderland of vast continents, towering mountains, immense plains, forests and rivers as compared to the tiny spaces and playgrounds of the British Isles themselves.

That is why it is not enough to know one's own bit, whether it be an English county or a huge Dominion. It is so much more interesting if we know something about other parts of the jigsaw puzzle and see how they fit into the pattern of our Empire and of the whole world. It is what is meant when it is said that no nation could understand itself without following history back into the past.

This gift book of yours tells how the King, as Duke of York, by his travels made history. It tells of the Coronation and its splendid ceremonies, because that is the greatest moment in every reign, when, as the Coronation ring symbolises, the Sovereign and the country are wedded to each other.

An old saying tells us that one cannot hate those whom one knows well. All coming-together, all meetings, if it is only through books and pictures, can lead to nothing but greater friendship, greater unity between all parts of the Empire: more than that, by means of the Empire, we can hope and pray, to a greater hope of peace throughout the world.

GEORGE VI

KING AND EMPEROR

George VI
King and Emperor

PLATE I

H.M. KING GEORGE VI.   [*Vandyk.*

PLATE II

H.M. QUEEN ELIZABETH.

[Vandyk.

PLATE III

PRINCESS ELIZABETH AND PRINCESS MARGARET ROSE RECEIVING
GIFTS AT THE DISABLED EX-SERVICEMEN'S EXHIBITION, 1933.

H.M. KING GEORGE VI ON HOLIDAY AT OSBORNE IN 1899.

PLATE IV

His Majesty King George VI and the Ex-King Edward VIII with Mr. Hansell, their Tutor, at Balmoral, 1911.

His Majesty (seated) among his fellow cadets.

GEORGE VI
KING AND EMPEROR

BY

MAJOR J. T. GORMAN

Author of
" Honour the King," etc.

LONDON
W. & G. FOYLE LTD.
CHARING CROSS ROAD, W.C.2

First Published 1937

CONTENTS

ILLUSTRATIONS

ILLUSTRATIONS

GEORGE VI, KING AND EMPEROR

CHAPTER ONE

HIS EARLY YEARS

IN the wide wooded grounds of Sandringham, near the lake, stands York Cottage, a country house almost as unpretending as its name. Here, on December 14th, 1895, was born Albert Frederick Arthur George, our present King, second son of the Duke and Duchess of Cornwall and York.

The Prince spent most of his childhood here, with those brothers and sister, who were such a happy simple family despite their Royalty. His grandparents' beautiful country home was close at hand, in the midst of heather and trees, while across the low Norfolk countryside came the salt wind from that grey North Sea, which the Sailor Prince was later to know so well when he helped to keep watch and ward there, in the grey ships of the Navy during the Great War.

Under their governess, Madame Bricka, Prince Albert was a pupil in a small nursery school and at an early age learnt part of a Royal child's duty—to look pleasant. They were attending some local entertainment and Prince Albert felt, and appeared, somewhat bored. Whereupon Princess Mary, sixteen months his junior, nudged him, whispering loudly: "Smile, keep on smiling!" And Prince Albert obeyed.

The young Prince was only five years old when his great-grandmother, Queen Victoria, died, and later in that same year, 1901, his parents went to Australia, to open the Federal Parliament, leaving their children in charge of his grandfather, King Edward VII, and Queen Alexandra. King Edward was devoted to Prince Albert, as was the boy's own father. Concerning the latter it is said that when the Prince was asked which parent he loved best, he answered thoughtfully: "Well, mother I think—but Daddy *spoils* us most."

When staying in London, the changing of the guard at St. James' Palace was a constant joy to the Royal children, and passers-by sometimes saw Prince Albert marching up and down in imitation of a Guard's sentry, whilst Princess Mary beat a drum.

It was of a certain lunch with King Edward on one of these London visits that an amusing story is told. Prince Albert, usually a shy, small boy, suddenly during the first course interrupted his grandfather's conversation and was gently reproved. Again he began: "But, Grandpapa——" and again was reminded that children should be seen, not heard. At the end of the meal, King Edward said kindly: "Now, what was it you wanted to say, my boy?" Prince Albert answered: "It's no good now. It was only to tell you there was a caterpillar in your salad, but you've eaten it."

There was a great reunion when the Duke and Duchess returned from their tour, and happy days with them at Sandringham, especially at Christmas, where the Royal children put up decorations and carried presents to all the villagers before receiving their own from the tree at night.

When nursery days were over, the Prince's real education began under Mr. H. B. Hansell, his tutor, with Monsieur Hua as French teacher. Prince Albert was an industrious boy, very persevering and steadily determined to learn, as he has remained all his life. Yet, at the same time, he was very fond of all outdoor games, especially cricket and football, with swimming in summer and skating on the Sandringham lake in winter.

The best cricketer of his family, Prince Albert, when staying at Windsor Castle, did the "hat trick," bowling with three successive balls King Edward VII, his own father and his elder brother. The ball used for this feat was mounted and given to the Royal Naval College at Dartmouth. Their Windsor cricket-field was the Royal Household ground at Frogmore, where Prince Albert also played against elevens from Eton and St. George's School, Windsor.

At Sandringham, besides cricket, he played football with the village boys, under the local schoolmaster, and so good a team resulted that they arranged fixtures against various private schools at Hunstanton and elsewhere.

In 1909, when he was thirteen years old, Prince Albert began his training for the Navy, first at Osborne, in the Isle of Wight, for two years, after which another two were spent at Dartmouth.

He was keen on his work, both the seamanship and the engineering sides: indeed, his determination to learn all he could in ships' engine-rooms has helped him since then to understand industrial machinery in factories, to know just why certain things happen and how various processes are brought about mechanically.

At Dartmouth, the Prince handled a boat better than any other cadet of his year, but he disliked the periodical examinations as much as many other boys, and they left him, as he says himself, "usually at the bottom of the lists." But he was thoroughly popular, both with his instructors and the other cadets, and described as "a good sport" in everything, work and games alike.

While Prince Albert was still in his first year at Osborne, King Edward VII died, and his own father became King as George V. But the death of his grandfather did not change the Prince's life very much, since it was intended that he should make a career in the Navy, as his father did before him. In 1911, wearing his cadet uniform, he was one of that State carriageful of young and laughing Royalties, who, as King George's family, attracted so much attention at the Coronation of their father and mother.

Later in the summer, Prince Albert was at Balmoral and is described as playing coon-can and dancing reels and flings; "a charming, unaffected boy of fifteen, looking well in his Highland evening dress," of Stuart tartan kilt, velvet coat and silver buttons and buckles.

In December, 1912, when he was just seventeen years old, Prince Albert passed out of Dartmouth and on January 18th, 1913, joined the county cruiser *Cumberland*, Captain Aubrey Smith; the cadet ship for that year, on which Prince Albert, with sixty other boys, was to gain practical sea experience before becoming a midshipman. The commander of *Cumberland* was an old friend of the Prince's, Commander H. Spencer Cooper; he had been one of his instructors at Dartmouth.

The cruise was a long and very interesting one, beginning with a visit to Teneriffe, Barbados, Martinique and many of the West Indian islands, including Jamaica. These were places which King George himself had visited many years before, when he and his elder brother, the Duke of Clarence, were midshipmen on H.M.S. *Bacchante*. Probably Prince Albert had read the published diary of that cruise and re-lived it again now, remembering his father's descriptions of the beautiful tropical islands, with their wonderful flowers, fruits, birds and butterflies; his visit to the Pitch Lake at Trinidad; how old negro women had greeted the brothers as "Queen Victoria's piccaninnies" and how they had bought pieces of coral and flying-fish wings for bookmarkers.

Afterwards *Cumberland* visited Cuba and Havana, then Bermuda, with its coral reefs and marvellous under-sea gardens. Here Prince Albert, who was such a keen boat-sailor, must have thoroughly enjoyed the wonderful sailing grounds of the Sounds, in the cedar-built Bermuda-rigged craft, so light that they almost seem to fly over the sea's surface.

Visits to Newfoundland and various Canadian ports completed the cruise and Prince Albert managed just to set foot in the United States by taking a trip to Niagara Falls. At the end of the tour the Prince was gazetted as midshipman to H.M.S. *Collingwood*, the flagship of Vice-Admiral Sir Stanley Colville, of the First Battle Squadron. He joined her at Rosyth in September, 1913.

In October, *Collingwood* sailed for the Mediterranean on a two months' cruise, visiting Malta and Egypt, where Prince Albert stayed with "K. of K." The great soldier had won his title in that same country just after the Prince was born.

On his new ship, Prince Albert was just as popular as he had been at the Royal Naval College and on *Cumberland*, and, like most popular people, he received a nickname by which he was always known, that of "Mr. Johnston." "Mr. Johnston" took an absolutely fair share in the ordinary ship's routine, up at six o'clock in the morning, attending classes in the schoolroom under the instructors, or taking his place in a working party with Naval ratings; eating a simple supper of bread, cheese, onions and beer and slinging up his own hammock at the end of the day.

Like his father before him, Prince Albert took a hand in coaling ship, although he never chanced to cause such consternation as King George did, when, as a young naval officer, in an Eastern Port, he appeared black from head to foot with coaldust, to interview a Turkish minister, who was horrified at seeing a Royal Prince in such a state.

Prince Albert kept up his Dartmouth reputation by coming out a constant winner in sailing races, and he won especial praise, too, for his skilful handling when in charge of the picket boat. In fact, he had the all-round character of doing well whatever he undertook, of being ready to work himself to a standstill for a pal, while, at the same time, as one of his brother-midshipmen said: "He was never one to push himself forward."

1913 passed, and now came the year which was to mean so much for Prince Albert as for many other boys. 1914 began with ordinary Fleet exercises at Portsmouth, after which Spring and Summer training took place at Lamlash, in the Isle of Arran. By June the Fleet was back once more in Devonport, making ready for that great July Review which, as it turned out, was to be only a dress rehearsal for war itself.

Directly after mobilisation, King George visited his fleet and came on board *Collingwood*. After inspecting the ship, he received all the officers on the quarter-deck, the captain introducing each in turn. Quite at the tail of the line came Prince Albert, to be formally presented to the father whom he had not seen for some months. But both were disciplined sailors, so not a word passed between them. Midshipman Prince Albert clicked heels and saluted Admiral of the Fleet King George; that was all and enough.

Not more than a month after the outbreak of war, Prince Albert received the first of those heavy blows which would have knocked out a less courageous boy again and again. He was taken suddenly ill and removed to the Hospital ship, *Rohilla*, then to an Aberdeen Nursing Home for an appendicitis operation.

This was not all the trouble, however, as was to be discovered later, and the Prince still suffered a great deal of pain after leaving the Home and being sent to the Admiralty to work in the Operations Department. But a shore job was unbearable to a young sailor who so longed to be on active service once more. After five weeks of office work, he pestered the Naval Medical Board to such an extent that in February, 1915, they allowed him to go to sea again. So "Mr. Johnston" rejoined *Collingwood* at Portsmouth, and on her went to the headquarters of the Grand Fleet at Scapa Flow.

That was only the beginning of the Prince's hard struggle against illness. For nine months he stuck to his ship, whilst she, with the rest of the Fleet, was keeping that grim watch in the North Sea. Then pain and weakness beat him for a time, and he went back to help his father in any way he could, with intervals in bed. But Prince Albert in the end got the chance he had fought for so hard and long: in May, 1916, he was allowed to rejoin *Collingwood*, just before the Battle of Jutland.

Collingwood was in the 5th Division of the First Battle Squadron of the Grand Fleet, forming line with *Colossus*, the flagship, *Neptune* and *St. Vincent* on that grey and gloomy afternoon of May 31st, when the report came through that the German High Sea Fleet had put out to sea.

Visibility was bad and growing worse with the failing light; only occasional gun-flashes could be seen through the gathering mists which hid everything beyond four miles. Prince Albert was serving in Number Two Turret, "A," 12-inch guns, the fore-turret of *Collingwood*, cooped up in that steel box, from which nothing could be seen and nothing heard, except the orders of an invisible gunnery officer through the telephone, giving range and direction on that invisible target. Then the great guns were swung and elevated into position; with their firing came the deafening crash, the tremendous recoil of that explosion and the turret filled with yellow smoke and acrid smells.

The gun-crew knew little more of the battle; hit or miss, they could not tell which: an enemy shell might shatter their turret at any moment. They just waited—but such waiting for part of a day and much of a night needed immense grit.

Collingwood's Division was in action for a good part of the engagement, even though the heaviest fighting was with the Battle Cruisers, Lord Beatty's great "Cats," *Lion*, *Tiger* and the rest. The Fifth Squadron was attacked by enemy destroyers, and immediately afterwards *Collingwood* and *Colossus* had a close-range duel with two German Battle Cruisers, possibly *Seydlitz* and *Derfflinger*, who escaped, damaged, into a smothering smoke-screen.

The battle lasted long enough to make it almost another "Glorious First of June"—that battle which was the most momentous fought by Britain at sea since Trafalgar itself. The

Prince had played his part in it bravely and well, though it is characteristic of him and of the Royal Navy in general that afterwards the officer of Number Two Turret remarked the only thing he particularly remembered about the battle was that "The Prince made cocoa as usual for me and the gun crew."

Second-lieutenant Prince Albert was mentioned in despatches for his services at Jutland, and one of the things he treasures most is the White Ensign which was flown by *Collingwood* in the action. No wonder that he looks back upon that experience with pride, and that in his first address to the Navy after his accession he said:

"It has been my privilege to serve as a Naval officer both in peace and in war: at Jutland, the greatest sea battle of modern times, I saw for myself in action the maintenance of those great traditions which are the inheritance of British seamen."

CHAPTER TWO

THE ROYAL MARRIAGE

ON his birthday, December 14th, 1916, His Royal Highness Prince Albert received the Order of the Garter; on December 14th, 1936, His Majesty King George VI made Her Majesty Queen Elizabeth a Lady of the Garter, as one of the first acts of his accession. But many things happened during the twenty years between these two dates.

After Jutland, the Prince went for a time to the battleship *Malaya*, then to a staff appointment on H.M.S. *Victory*—with the understanding that he was to be summoned back to the Fleet immediately if there was the chance of another battle. But his illness grew worse, until in November, 1917, a most serious operation became necessary. Once it was over, however, Prince Albert steadily improved, and from that time his health has been splendid.

Early in 1918 the Prince left the Navy for good, and entered the Royal Naval Air Service. He went for training to Cranwell, and showed just the same perseverance and keenness as he had in his sea-going days; the same determination to do his job well. This was especially seen when the time came for him to make his first flight, an experience to which he never pretended to look forward.

The date chosen was wet and windy, not at all a good flying day and the commanding officer, feeling rather uneasy, suggested to the Prince that he should put off the flight. But the young airman was decided: "I don't want to go up at all," he confessed honestly. "But I shan't like it a bit better if I wait till to-morrow, so let's get it over to-day."

The flight was made successfully, and the Prince acquitted himself well. Shortly afterwards when the R.N.A.S. was merged in the Royal Air Force, he was appointed to the staff of Lord Trenchard, in France, and flew across the channel to join his chief at Nancy in time to see the end of the war on the Western Front. During this period an amusing incident occurred: the Prince happened to go into a strange aerodrome and made

PLATE V

AN AERIAL VIEW OF WINDSOR CASTLE: HISTORIC HOME OF THE KINGS OF ENGLAND.
St. George's Chapel in the foreground.

PLATE VI

GLAMIS CASTLE, THE ANCESTRAL HOME OF QUEEN ELIZABETH.

ROYAL LODGE, WINDSOR: THE COUNTRY HOME OF THE ROYAL FAMILY.

his way to the officers' mess. An airman who chanced to be there noticed the rainbow-rows of medal-ribbons on the youthful newcomer's tunic and remarked:

"Hullo! A bit young, aren't you, to have collected so many decorations!"

"Well," the Prince answered, smiling, "sometimes these things can't be helped, you know."

After the Armistice, Prince Albert chose to stay with his comrades in Belgium instead of coming home for Christmas; on November 22nd, wearing the Royal Air Force uniform, he was with his namesake, King Albert, when he made a triumphal re-entry into Brussels, his capital.

At the beginning of 1919, the Prince went to Croydon to finish his air-training, and there qualified as a pilot, making a solo flight over London. He was exceedingly popular with both officers and mechanics, and here, as at Cranwell, was generally known as "Bertie." It is related that one of the mechanics was noticed to be taking the most extraordinary pains with the cleaning and overhauling of an Avro machine. On comment being made the man said, "Of course I am! Aren't I getting this 'bus ready for Bertie to go mooching over the chimney-pots?"

The Prince's active career in the Air Force ended in the autumn of 1919, when, like many other lads whose education was interrupted by the war, he went for a year to Cambridge. Although entered at Trinity College, he, with his brother, Prince Henry, lived outside in a private house with Wing-Commander Louis Greig, one of Prince Albert's greatest friends. Characteristically the Prince took up those special studies which he thought would be most useful in the future—Political Economy, modern history and civics, and worked very steadily. But he tells the story himself of how on one occasion he was "progged," run in, that is, by the Proctors and fined six shillings and eight-pence for the terrible offence against university rules of smoking a pipe while wearing his cap and gown.

The Prince left Cambridge in 1920, and in the Birthday Honours of that year was created Duke of York. But just before this, something happened which we may be sure the Prince looks back upon as quite the most important as well as the happiest event of his whole life.

A ball was given during the London season and there Prince Albert saw a dainty, blue-eyed, black-haired girl who was described to him as one of the best dancers in the room. But the Prince had seen Lady Elizabeth Bowes-Lyon before and remembered it, although on that thirteen-years-ago occasion she was then only five years old.

This time, he was no longer a shy ten-year-old schoolboy, but a grown man, who, then and there, knew that he was in love, and meant to marry this girl and no other; this youngest daughter of the ancient Scottish house of Strathmore.

Prince Albert has always been one to know his own mind and keep to it. That same summer he went with Queen Mary to Glamis Castle, where little Lady Elizabeth, her mother being ill, acted as a most gracious hostess, and showed the young Prince all the beauties of the haunted ancient house and its lovely surroundings. That visit strengthened Prince Albert's resolve, but, always shy and diffident, he resolved to wait until Lady Elizabeth knew him better.

At the marriage of his sister, Princess Mary, in 1922, Lady Elizabeth was a bridesmaid, and people began to wonder—and hope. But it was only after a quiet and steadfast courtship of more than three years, that the announcement was made at last in January, 1923, that King George had given his consent to the marriage of his "dearly beloved son" to Lady Elizabeth Angela Marguerite Bowes-Lyon.

There was Empire-wide delight and satisfaction: everybody rejoiced that a British girl had been chosen by the British Prince —and that delight and satisfaction has only deepened during the past fourteen years.

The engagement was not a long one: it was to be an April wedding, and the engagement-ring was made of deep blue sapphires, one of the lucky stones for that month. When the date was fixed for April 26th, a very important document was prepared—the marriage licence. This was "engrossed," that is, written entirely by hand, and it took an old and experienced clerk three whole days to write it in Old English lettering, using twenty quill pens of different thicknesses, some from swans, some from geese, on a piece of parchment nearly a yard square with especially prepared black ink. During all this time the clerk, a Mr. Bull, worked in a locked room.

In March, the engaged couple went for a short visit to Glamis Castle, and on their way had a day's shopping in Edinburgh, and personally chose a design for their wonderful wedding-cake, which was to be in four tiers with the coats of arms of the two families as the chief ornaments.

They ended this very busy day in a way which any of their present boy-subjects would appreciate by going to the Rugby Football match, England *v.* Scotland, and the huge Scottish crowds assembled there nearly as much to see and greet the Prince and Lady Elizabeth, their fellow country-woman, as to watch the game itself.

England won—and Prince Albert, who had wanted his wife-to-be to see Scotland the victors, is said to have remarked that for once in his life he felt quite unpatriotic.

Then Lady Elizabeth went back to her father's London home, in Bruton Street, and awaited the huge flood of letters and presents which had already begun to flow in, presents from all parts of the world and all kinds of people. Almost all the letters of thanks were written by Lady Elizabeth or the Prince with their own hands—and that alone was a big task.

One of these presents was something which showed the bride's thoughtfulness and kind heart. A needlework competition had been arranged to raise money for the national orthopædic hospital, where so many boys and girls, who have never been able to walk since they were born, are given what is almost like new lives.

In order to make the public interested in this competition and increase the amount of entrance money, Lady Elizabeth asked that the winning piece of needlework might be one of her wedding presents, and this was done, to the great good of the children in the hospital and the pride of the prizewinner who had embroidered the lovely household linen.

It is only possible to mention just a few more of the wedding presents, but some of them were very interesting—the ancient clock, originally made for George IV and sent by the City of Glasgow, which played a military march at noon every day —except on Sundays. When the march begins a door opens at one side of the dial, which represents Whitehall in 1804 and a procession of Horse Guards with the King and Royal Family of that date moves across.

The needlemakers' company sent Lady Elizabeth a thousand

gold-eyed needles in a beautiful case—and one wonders whether Her Majesty the Queen has yet been able to use them all.

Disabled soldiers of the Blighty Works at Slateford sent tartan travelling rugs woven with the Royal monogram and a crown; the Emperor of Japan marvellous china vases. Probably, Prince Albert valued more than anything the lovely miniature portrait of his bride which Lady Strathmore had had painted for him, but one of the very nicest presents of all was given *by* as well as *to* the Prince. This was a cheque for £2,500, collected as a wedding gift, but Prince Albert divided it between five great cities, Edinburgh, Glasgow, Cardiff, York and Bradford, to provide treats for poor children, and he also sent for each huge party a wonderful wedding-cake, four feet high.

At last the great day came, a real English April day, grey and rainy at first, but bursting out into glorious sunshine, just as the bride left her father's house, looking a true fairy Princess, with diamonds and lace in her hair and a white ermine coat covering her exquisite wedding-gown. It was a very "thoughtful" wedding-dress, too: Lady Elizabeth wanted to encourage British industry, so her frock was covered with Nottingham-made lace instead of the priceless heirloom lace which she might have worn.

The grey walls of Westminster Abbey never saw a lovelier pageant; a grander display of beautiful dresses and gorgeous uniforms. All the services were represented in the wedding group, for the King wore Admiral's dress, the bridegroom that of the Royal Air Force and his brothers the uniforms of their regiments.

It was a White Rose wedding, and the bride and her eight bridesmaids, two of them children, were themselves like a nosegay of snowy flowers, all in white, with wreaths of white rosebuds. Lady Elizabeth carried the wedding bouquet which had been given to her by the Worshipful Company of Gardeners, made up of white roses and white heather, and as she entered the Abbey, on her father's arm, she turned aside and very gently and gravely laid this beautiful symbol of her own happiness and gain as a tribute upon the grave of the Unknown Warrior who had given all for his country.

Then, with the golden processional cross carried before her, the dainty white figure moved slowly up the aisle towards where Prince Albert stood waiting, with the Archbishop of

PLATE VII

BUCKINGHAM PALACE AND THE QUEEN VICTORIA MEMORIAL, LONDON.

ST. JAMES'S PALACE LONDON.

Plate VIII

The Wedding Day of Their Majesties, April 26th, 1923.
King George V and Queen Mary and the parents of the Bride, the Earl and Countess of Strathmore.

Canterbury, who was to marry them. And everyone noticed, as a beautiful sign, that just as she reached the steps and the bridegroom came forward to meet her with a smile, a shaft of sunshine shone down upon their heads through a near-by window.

After the ceremony was over, all the bridal party went straight to Buckingham Palace except the newly-married pair, who rode in their glass coach along a roundabout route, especially chosen so that they might be seen by as many people as possible. Side by side they sat and hand-in-hand, smiling and bowing to the huge crowds who waved and cheered all the time. Only once was there a serious moment: this was when the shining coach drew up for a moment beside the Cenotaph, while the Duke rose and saluted and the newly-made Duchess sat with her head bowed.

So by Piccadilly and Constitution Hill, where banks of daffodils and crocuses blazed in greeting, they came back to the Palace, to toasts and the cutting of the immense cake with the bridegroom's sword, and an appearance on the balcony to delight the waiting people, before they drove away amidst a shower of white rose-petals to Polesden Lacy House, in Surrey, which had been lent them for the first part of the honeymoon.

There, near Dorking and Box Hill, they stayed for a short time before going on to Glamis, where the great beacon was lighted in their honour and the Duchess' own Girl Guides were waiting to welcome their District Commissioner to her own County and Country.

Just a few weeks were spent there, for Royalties are busy people and cannot spare much time, even for honeymoons: then after a very short interval at Frogmore, near Windsor, the Duke and Duchess went to the house which was to be their home for a time: White Lodge, in Richmond Park, which had also been Queen Mary's home, both as a child and after her marriage, until just before the birth of Prince Albert.

It is a pleasant country house, with the ancient trees of the Park all about it; inside, Queen Mary herself had re-arranged the rooms, adding their new possessions to the old State furniture. Here the Duke and Duchess lived for more than eighteen months, although part of this time was spent in visits to Scotland, Northern Ireland and to represent the King and act as "Koom" and "Koomitsa"—godfather and godmother at the christening of the eldest child of King Alexander and Queen Marie of Yugoslavia.

CHAPTER THREE

THE EMPIRE TOURS

"I RETURN a thorough optimist. When one has seen how the grit and creative purpose of our kinsmen overseas have triumphed over the most tremendous difficulties, it is impossible to despair of the future of the British race."

Those hopeful and cheering words were spoken by the Duke of York at the Guildhall after he returned from a World Empire tour in 1927—for we must not forget that our King has already visited many of the Dominions. The first tour was in 1924, when the Duke and Duchess went to Kenya Colony, Uganda and the Sudan, although it was chiefly a shooting and sight-seeing holiday, with only a few official engagements. This being so, it was not a "warship" tour: they sailed in the P. and O. *Mulbera* and landed at Mombasa on December 22nd, where a flag flew with "Welcome to Kenya!" They were greeted by what was perhaps the native idea of "waits"; Kikuya stilt-walkers dancing and singing, with gilt crowns in which were stuck lighted candles. After this the Duke and Duchess were given an elephant's tusk with an Arabic address of welcome inside and a gold coin on a red ribbon.

Then came the wonderful journey to Nairobi, past 17,000 feet high Mount Kenya, through the game country, where herds of giraffe, antelope, wildebeeste and even elephants could be seen from the train, with the other huge mountain, Kilimanjaro, in the distance. Christmas was spent at Nairobi, capital of Kenya, where they went to church and the Duchess was given a prayer-book in the native language, Kiswahili.

After this, came the thrilling part of the tour, when they went on *safari*, into camp, that is, for big-game shooting and photography. Here the Duchess proved herself a thorough sportswoman, quite enjoying the out-door meals and rough life under canvas at Siola, and actually killing a rhinoceros herself with one shot. Several times they were in dangerous situations; once a rhino, already wounded by the Duke, charged him, and was barely thirty yards off when killed by a second shot. On

New Year's Day the Duke shot a lioness, and was immediately attacked by two furious buffalo, fortunately bringing both down with two successive shots.

But it was the beautiful scenery, the strange people which pleased the Duchess more than the "heads" they collected: she was sorry to leave the wilds, when the time came to go on to. Uganda, going by water to Entebbe, the British capital, on the shores of the huge lake Victoria Nyanza. Next day they visited Kampala, the near-by native city, built—like ancient Rome—on seven hills, on two of which stand the English and Roman Catholic Cathedrals. Here they were entertained by the native King Daudi, a fine sportsman and loyal ally, and received many gifts, including two magnificent tusks, before visiting the source of the Nile at Ripon Falls and going on to the Semliki valley to complete their hunting experiences and go a-fishing on Lake Albert Nyanza.

A rare white rhinoceros was the Duchess' chief prize here, after which they travelled a thousand miles along the Nile into the Sudan, going ashore sometimes to take the photographs which are now a constant interest to the little Princesses.

At Khartoum—where the streets of the new city are laid out to form the Union Jack—there was much excitement, with illuminations and entertainments, and the desert said farewell in a blinding sandstorm, which detained them on the Suez Canal for twelve hours.

April saw the Duke and Duchess home again, and just a year later, in 1926, came the birth of Princess Elizabeth, the world's best-known baby, who was barely eight months old when her parents set off in January, 1927, for their second and greatest tour, this time to perform a most important duty in the Empire's service.

The first Federal Parliament of Australia was to sit in the new Government House at Canberra and the Duke had been asked to perform the opening ceremony. So the Duchess left the tiny baby in charge of her two grandmothers and set out with her husband to the other side of the world on board H.M.S. *Renown*.

Las Palmas, in the Canary Islands, was their first stopping-place, after which they set off across the Atlantic to Kingston, Jamaica, and from there crossed the American continent through the Panama Canal. On February 1st came the important occasion of "Crossing the Line," and although the Duke protested that he had already been through the ceremonies on the African journey, the crew of the *Renown* decided that a passenger liner did not count, so he laughingly allowed himself to be lathered with a bill-poster's brush, shaved with a huge wooden razor and afterwards ducked, when King Neptune and his followers came on board.

The Duchess received the Order of the Golden Mermaid, and afterwards, when members of the crew gave a cabaret entertainment, the Royal guests arrived amid much laughter in a comic motor-car, made from the wheel-chair which had been used by one of the suite who injured his leg.

Renown stopped for oil at Nukohiva, one of the Marquesas islands, and here the Duke and Duchess had two interesting experiences. The first was a "Pig Dance," the men who performed this grunting all the time like wild boars: the other was the introduction of the Duke to an ancient man who had once been a real cannibal.

Suva, in the Fiji Islands, was the next port of call, with a truly Royal welcome from the Fijians. Rabu Popi, the native chief, presented a *Tabua*, or sperm whale's tooth, as a sign of loyalty, brought in a model canoe which was dragged by two long lines of Fijian women across the Government House lawn, with a red coral crown for the Duchess. Afterwards the Duke drank the chief's health in a bowl of *kava*, the native liquor, and the Royal pair were escorted back to *Renown* that night by magnificent-looking torch-bearers and spearmen, chanting farewell.

Auckland gave them a wild welcome to New Zealand, and a month was spent in the two islands, the first visit being to the weird Rotorua region, where volcanoes and warm springs provide a constant natural supply of H and C, or absolutely boiling water for bathing and cooking. Here there is a settlement of Maoris, the splendid natives of New Zealand, whose song of greeting began: "Son, welcome—Daughter of an honoured house, welcome, welcome!" The Duke began his answer with the Maori word: "Tenakouton"—greeting to you all; and ended with: "Kia Ora"—good luck!

Then they saw the *Haka*, or warrior dance, and the *Poi*, or

PLATE IX

THEIR MAJESTIES, IN A GAME OF DECK QUOITS ON DECK OF H.M.S. "RENOWN," 1927.

HIS MAJESTY AND PRINCESS MARY ON THE ALPINE RAILWAY, EARL'S COURT EXHIBITION, 1913.

PLATE X.

AT SUVA, FIJI. PRESENTING A "TABUA" (TOOTH OF THE SPERM WHALE) AS A SYMBOL
OF HOMAGE AND AFFECTION, 1927.

AT THE PARADE OF BOY SCOUTS AND GIRL GUIDES, ADELAIDE, AUSTRALIA:
The King gives the Scout Handshake.

PLATE XI

CANBERRA, AUSTRALIA.
Their Majesties Opening the First Federal Parliament, May 9th, 1927.

Plate XII

His Majesty Landing a Shark in the Bay of Islands, New Zealand, 1927.

Their Majesties and Princess Elizabeth, 1926.

girls' dance with flax balls, and were given several beautiful native articles, especially a Royal cloak made of kiwi feathers, supposed to bring good luck, which the Duke wore during the ceremony.

It was a blow to loyal New Zealand when the Duchess had a severe attack of tonsillitis, and the Duke was obliged to finish the tour alone. At Ashburton, in South Island, where the famous "Canterbury Lamb" comes from, the queerest of decorations had been erected—two fine sheep's carcases, swinging between poles, which gradually began to frizzle in the sun's heat. Everywhere there were cheers and shouts of: "We want the Duchess!" and "Three cheers for the baby at home," and at Invercargill the children had all subscribed pennies to buy the biggest "kewpie" in New Zealand as a gift for Princess Elizabeth.

Another New Zealand present for the baby princess had been an enormous doll brought to the Duchess at Auckland by two tiny Brownies, scarcely bigger than their gift. Yet another was a bunch of white heather, given with a "tiki," or greenstone mascot, by four little girls, who also presented the Duke and Duchess with tufts of white feathers from the sacred *Nuia* bird, to be worn in their hats. Just before leaving New Zealand the Duke received another doll in a cot, and delighted the children who gave it by carefully tucking in the blankets.

During his solitary half of the tour the Duke made serious enquiries into the state of housing in New Zealand and the trade conditions. On his way to Christchurch, too, he thoroughly enjoyed taking the place of the engine-driver on the Royal train and driving the engine through what is supposed to be the longest tunnel in the British Empire, arriving at the further end greasy, hot and dirty, but well pleased with himself. This delighted the New Zealanders, but everywhere there were the same shouts of welcome, the feeling which was expressed in the inscription upon a huge flag displayed at one town: "Tell the King we're loyal."

The Duchess was nearly well again by the time that the Duke rejoined *Renown* at Auckland, but New Zealand gave them rather a rough good-bye, for the weather was so stormy that the Duke was obliged to take a big jump to reach the warship from the rocking tug alongside, much to the anxiety of the Duchess, who watched from the deck.

But Australia welcomed them in brilliant sunshine as they steamed into lovely Sydney Harbour, with two big flying-boats overhead, striped with the Commonwealth red, white and blue. Amid silence *Renown* moved to her moorings: then as the ship's band struck up the National Anthem, there was thunder of guns, pealing of bells, hooting of syrens and the cheers of thousands echoing to every bay and cove of the harbour. On shore it was the same—especially where the boys of Sydney's biggest school were assembled to shout: "Greetings from Grammar! Grammar sends greetings to Princess Elizabeth!"

It was said that a famous Australian general actually climbed a lamp-post to get a glimpse of the "smiling Duchess," as she was already called in the Antipodes, and everywhere the "Cornstalks" yelled: "We want the Duke—we want the Duchess!" Here at Sydney, too, there was the first "Public Reception" as they were called, the crowd marching by, three or four abreast, so that as many as possible might have a good view of the Royalties. Several times this procession was held up: once when a pair of baby twins stopped in their perambulator to give the Duchess a threepenny-bit for Princess Elizabeth's money-box.

After visiting the Blue Mountains and the famous Jenolan caves—and incidentally seeing a real wild kangaroo bound across the road in front of their car—the Duke and Duchess went north to Queensland and Brisbane, through miles of wonderful wheat country to a region of pineapples and other tropical fruit.

On the way, they stopped for a "billy tea" picnic and to see some of the finest horsemen "down under," riding wild horses, or "brumbies," and cutting-out cattle at the annual championships. There was a native "corroboree" as well, with exhibitions of boomerang and "waddie," or stick throwing, with dances given by the blackfellows—and the Duchess acquired an addition to Princess Elizabeth's presents in the shape of a huge teddy-bear.

A very pleasant event was a Ball in a shearing-shed, where fifteen hundred people were assembled and formed a huge circle to watch the Duke and Duchess dance together—a sight well-worth seeing, for both loved dancing. Before they left Brisbane for Tasmania, the Duke and Duchess found themselves honoured with the name of "Diggers," that true title of comrade-ship amongst the "Aussies."

Tasmania was determined to give them a real island welcome: at beautiful Hobart Town, with another wonderful harbour, two triumphal arches were erected, one entirely of rosy apples, the other of stacked and packed wool, in which a recess was cut to show a man shearing a sheep. There was a great assembly of ex-servicemen, and one old soldier presented the Duke with a very curious walking-stick, made from the top-branch of a very rare kind of pine-tree which grows only in the island. This was not all: the April birthday of Princess Elizabeth was near, and Tasmanian children, to show they had not forgotten it, brought a lovely set of inlaid doll's bedroom furniture, made from Tasmanian blackwood.

The Duke and Duchess arrived at Melbourne in time to share in the National Day of Remembrance on April 25th, Anzac Day, when thirty thousand ex-servicemen, led by twenty-nine V.C.s, marched past the Cenotaph erected on the steps of Parliament House where the Duke stood.

This was the serious part of the Melbourne visit, but there were plenty of amusing things, too, like the University students' "rag," when they surrounded the Duke in the most comical "animal" dresses—sheep, cows, pigs, goats, kangaroos and so on, with a big poster: "If he won't come to the country, the country must come to him."

From Melbourne the Duke and Duchess visited Ballarat, where the great gold fields were discovered nearly a hundred years ago, and here the Duchess was much interested to see the wonderful work of the "Lucas Girls." This is an avenue, stretching away for fourteen miles, silent and shaded by more than three thousand trees. Each of these trees is a living memorial, for each bears the name of a soldier or nurse who died in the war, and the money to plant them was collected by five hundred "Lucas Girls."

Crossing the frontier into South Australia they visited the charming town of Adelaide, and were greeted at its outskirts by a crowd of factory girls, who threw such volleys of yellow and red paper streamers into and round the Royal motor-car that it was quite a business to disentangle it. In the town itself, twelve thousand school children had prepared a really beautiful

19

display. They were arranged to form an enormous living map of Australia, with the words "Welcome" written across it in different coloured letters.

And now the time was near for the most important event of the Royal visit to Australia, the event on May 9th to which Australians in hundreds of thousands hurried to camp on the hills and plain where the capital city of Canberra was just beginning to grow, where a few newly-raised buildings rose among all the tents, which had sprung up mushroom-like in a night.

The great white Parliament House, in its green setting, waited with closed doors which the Duke was to open. The Royal pair drove up in an open carriage, drawn by four horses with out-riders and postillions, the Duke wearing naval uniform: they were welcomed by the "National Anthem," the first verse being sung by Dame Nellie Melba, the world-famous Australian singer, whose name was taken from her native town —Melbourne.

Fifty thousand people joined in, and at the same time a cloud of carrier pigeons rose into the sky, taking aerial messages all over the Commonwealth. The Duke unlocked the doors with a golden key and, passing inside, unveiled a statue of his father, King George V, who on this very same day, May 9th, 1901, had opened the first Federal Parliament of Australia. King George had sent greetings by his son, which the Duke now gave, together with his father's present to the new Parliament Buildings of two despatch cases, exactly like those used in the British House of Commons. In an excellent speech the Duke spoke of the building of Canberra: "a great landmark in the history of Australia."

As he ended, buglers blew a fanfare and a salute of twenty-one guns told that the ceremony was over. Next day the Duchess planted two trees—one, a willow, from Kew Gardens, in London —in what will some day be the great central park of Canberra.

This was almost the end of the Australian tour; only the West still remained to be visited, and they had no warmer welcome anywhere in the Antipodes than that at Perth from three thousand returned soldiers. As the Royal pair entered the theatre that evening, the Duke was greatly delighted at being greeted with: "Who's your Lady Friend?" and "We love a Lassie—a bonnie Hieland Lassie," sung with much emphasis.

Plate XIII

Their Majesties at Sea.
H.M.S. "Renown" during their Australian Tour, 1927.

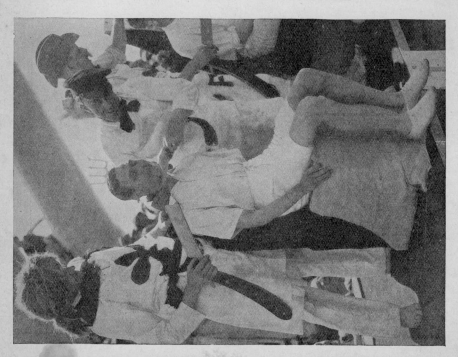

H.M.S. "Renown." "Crossing the Line" Ceremony.
Lathered and shaved preparatory to the Ducking, 1927.

PLATE XIV

A FAMILY GROUP.

PRINCE EDWARD.
One year old son of the Duke and Duchess of Kent; nephew of King George VI. 1936.

On May 12th they left Australia, as the Duke said: "With very great regret," and to the sounds of the Australian Navy's last salute, a chorus of "cooees" and the singing of "Auld Lang Syne," and "The girl I left behind me," *Renown* steamed away on the return voyage.

Midway between Perth and Mauritius, 1,100 miles from the nearest land, on May 26th, Queen Mary's birthday, an incident occurred which might have been very unpleasant. Fire broke out on *Renown* and could not be got under for more than twelve hours, though the ship hove to and all hands fought the flames grimly. Perhaps it is hardly necessary to say—knowing our Royal Family—that neither the Duke nor Duchess seemed the least bit disturbed, although naturally everyone was relieved when at midnight the danger was past and it was possible to go to bed in peace.

At Mauritius, a picturesque island, with its two towering central peaks, amidst the forests and crags of which it is sometimes rumoured that living specimens of that so-called extinct bird the Dodo may still exist, the Duke and Duchess received some beautiful presents, the most unusual being a silver four-inch-to-the-mile map of the island with the roads marked in gleaming threads, the four lighthouses with rubies, Port Louis, the capital, by a sapphire, and the fifty sugar factories with diamonds.

Indeed by now *Renown* was something between a Noah's Ark and a toyshop, it carried so large a collection of animals and birds, such a vast number of toys for Princess Elizabeth.

Up the coast of Africa, through the Red Sea and Suez Canal, with last stops at Malta and Gibraltar—all new to the Duchess though not to the Duke—and then the arrival at Spithead on June 27th; the reunion in London with their little daughter after six months spent in encompassing the world.

CHAPTER FOUR

THE KING HIMSELF

OUR King once described himself as "a very ordinary person, if people only knew it," But that is no reason why he should not be a very extra-ordinary Sovereign. After all, it is said that genius itself is only doing common things uncommonly well, which rather applies to King George.

He is very thorough in all he does, very persevering, not apt to give up what he has once undertaken, and not at all easily discouraged, as he showed early in life during his long fight against illness throughout the war. He showed it, too, in his determination to make himself a good speaker, to overcome the slight impediment which made him at one time nervous of saying anything in public. Many boys would have let it go at that, have decided just to put up with it, but not so Prince Albert, as he then was: he intended to be cured, and cured he was, although it meant doing wearisome exercises for years. In the end he won, and now speaks well in public and with little or no hesitation. Only those who suffer in the same way will quite know what grit it needed to get over that obstacle.

A nice story is told about this voice training of the King's. When very small, Princess Elizabeth firmly refused to open her mouth so that her teeth might be cleaned. Finally she was persuaded by her father saying: "Now open it, just like Daddy in the morning, when he does his exercises"—and from that time she treated tooth-brushing as a great joke.

This incident shows, too, King George's love and understanding of children. He has always been the friend and companion of his small daughters, and whenever possible he and Princess Elizabeth ride together in the Great Park at Windsor, while she likes nothing so much as to watch her father, when he is spending some leisure time in his workshop with the latest wireless gadgets, or in taking an old clock to pieces and putting its works in order, which is one of his hobbies.

The King was one of the earliest wireless "fans"; like most of his boy subjects-to-be, he would busy himself for hours with his radio set in those experimental days, and he is still keenly interested in any new wireless developments, such as television.

It is the same with photography and kinematography: he soon discovers all about the workings of any camera, and became very keen on the cine-kodak soon after its invention, taking films at his Boys' Camp and other places, to amuse the little Princesses. King George, in fact, is an all-round handy-man, especially in anything connected with machinery. He showed mechanical tastes at Dartmouth and Cranwell, where ship and aeroplane engines were concerned, and no chauffeur could teach him much about the running repairs to a car.

He has driven railway engines in New Zealand and elsewhere —probably realising a youthful ambition shared by many other boys: on one occasion in Glasgow he piloted a tram-car through crowded streets, and he would probably be equally ready to drive a traction engine, a tractor or a tank if he got the chance.

Like most of his family, the King has a wonderful memory, and has often taken people by surprise when he recognised them after many years. But no one should suppose that all Royalties have this gift by nature, and that they take no trouble about remembering things or persons. Memory can be trained, like every other power we possess, and those born in high places know how important and useful it is to them.

It was for this reason that King George, when Duke of York, kept a most careful diary while abroad on his world tour, making notes of all important conversations and of any interesting people and things he came across. Then he has the habit of asking questions: when he goes over a factory or institution of any kind, he is not content to look at the outside of things. He wants to know all about processes and methods of work: in fact, as one business manager said: "Of all the visitors we have had here I never met one who asked more sensible questions, or showed greater understanding. He does like getting to the bottom of things." And it is just that liking which makes him so thorough.

It is the same when he visits hospitals—which is often, because he is the President of many. But here something is added, perhaps because of his own experience of illness. A little fellow in a children's hospital which the King was visiting had just come round after an operation and the King sat by him for a few minutes. After he had gone, the boy said: "Lumme, 'e knows! 'E said 'e'd felt just like what I did, sick an' all that. Ain't 'e *nice* ?"

That is the same thing in different words which King George said himself, speaking of sympathy: "It is personal contact and understanding: you must be able to share the joys and troubles of those you are trying to help."

At one time, King George used to be spoken of as the "Serious Prince," and perhaps in some ways he seems quieter and graver than his brothers, partly because as a boy he was very shy. But he has a great sense of humour, as all his friends and relations know—as the boys at his camp, too, could tell you. When he is playing games, not only the real serious kind, but ridiculous card or round games with his children, he is very boyish himself and during his tours abroad he was ready for any kind of joke on land or on board-ship. In fact, some of his suite thought the Duke rather *too* ready, when he produced ridiculous snapshots which he had taken of them!

Once in New Zealand where a huge crowd was waiting for him at a railway station, he managed to slip down on to the permanent way from one of the end carriages, while the train was still moving, and then, unnoticeable in a plain flannel suit, mixed with the crowd on the platform, waving his hat and cheering *himself*, as the train came to a standstill in the station.

As a matter of fact, both he and the Queen thoroughly enjoy a joke against themselves: during this tour they took great delight in collecting cuttings from newspapers, with stories and anecdotes about their own doings. These the King stuck into a scrapbook, which he labelled: "Things which did *not* happen to Us."

Like the Queen, King George is very fond of reading, but while her favourite books are historical, or the lives of famous people, the King loves "thrillers" of the Edgar Wallace kind, as a change from the stiff works about industrial and economic subjects which he studies so that he may know how to rule his subjects the better.

Besides the wireless, he likes listening to the gramophone, and has a fine collection of all kinds of records—especially dance music and musical comedy, the latter being the kind of play he likes best. And when it comes to the Pictures, it *has* been said

PLATE XV

KING GEORGE VI (WHEN DUKE OF YORK) RIDING WITH THE LATE KING GEORGE V AND
THE PRINCE OF WALES AT THE TROOPING OF THE COLOUR, HORSE GUARDS PARADE, 1928.

HIS MAJESTY (WEARING R.A.F. UNIFORM) WITH THE DUKE OF GLOUCESTER, AT THE
TROOPING THE COLOUR, 1928.

PLATE XVI

PRINCESS ELIZABETH AND HER MOTHER, 1930.

PRINCESS ELIZABETH RIDING IN WINDSOR GREAT PARK WITH HER FATHER, ON HER TENTH
BIRTHDAY.

that he shares his daughter's fondness for "Mickey Mouse" and "Silly Symphonies," like many of his subjects, old and young.

The King has a great love of animals, especially of dogs, which go to him as a trusted friend. Perhaps his favourites are the beautiful golden Labrador retrievers of which he owns several, but all kinds of dogs abound in this home, especially at Royal Lodge, Windsor, and when the King is at work, one of them is almost always sitting at his feet.

He takes a great interest in all his daughters' pets: when *Renown* came back from the Antipodes loaded with animals and birds of all kinds—including twenty parrots!—he and the Queen were much distressed when some of the creatures fell sick during the voyage, still more so when an opossum and a wallaby died and a green parakeet flew away out of a cabin porthole.

That is why the young Princesses consider rightly that they have the best sort of father: he shares their interests—and not in a superior grown-up manner. Life at Royal Lodge or at 145 Piccadilly has always been much like that lived in thousands of happy households all over Great Britain, quite simple and homely. Royal Lodge, especially, is just a charming country house: not a bit "grand." It is in Windsor Great Park, and within its grounds is the little Royal Chapel of All Saints, where the King and his family often go to church. Royal Lodge was built in 1814 for the Prince Regent and in those days it had a thatched roof and rose-covered verandah. Now it has been rebuilt and the big conservatory pulled down where Queen Victoria—then just the present age of Princess Elizabeth—used to listen to the concerts given by King George IV's band. There is a lovely garden, and from the terrace a most beautiful view of Windsor Castle, the Long Walk and the "Copper Horse" statue of George III.

An even simpler home is 145 Piccadilly, from which the Royal family moved to Buckingham Palace—probably with a good many regrets. But the big Palace gardens will make a splendid playground for the Princesses, and wherever they may go, a "home" will go with them, for that is, after all, made by people themselves, not the places they live in.

At Buckingham Palace, the King no doubt will use the study and library which was once his father's; while at "145" he went daily to work in plainly furnished offices nearby at 11,

Grosvenor Crescent, since the Piccadilly house had not enough space.

It is curious that of the various Royal residences, it is just that one which is the official Palace, which has been rarely used by our kings and queens themselves since 1685. Ambassadors from foreign countries are said to be sent to "The Court of St. James," but the King does not now live in St. James's Palace, although many Government officials have rooms there. Yet Accession and Coronation proclamations are always made in one of the many courtyards of that old red brick building, which has seen so many strange and historic happenings outside and inside its walls.

Buckingham Palace has only been a Royal residence for about a hundred years—and Marble Arch, which, as is known, stands in quite a different part of London, was *meant* to be the Palace entrance. The huge house is full of wonderful furniture, pictures and china, and the State rooms are a splendid sight when prepared for a Court, or Banquet or Ball. But one very interesting part of Buckingham Palace can be seen by any boy or girl who gets permission on a certain day in each week. It is the Royal Mews, in Buckingham Palace Road, where the King's horses are kept, including the "Windsor Greys," who draw the State Coach, as well as many curiosities in the way of harness and carriages. Probably a new horse is stabled there now, on which Princess Elizabeth will ride with her father in the Row when they are in London, as the Princess Royal used to ride with *her* father, King George V.

There is one part of Buckingham Palace where both Princess Elizabeth and Princess Margaret have already been seen many times, beginning with that day when the elder Princess, as a tiny baby was held up in her mother's arms to be seen by a delighted crowd on the return of the Duke and Duchess of York from their world tour. This is the famous balcony above the front courtyard, where the Royal Family have again and again made an appearance on great occasions in answer to the cheers of the people and where in past years the heads of the Princesses hardly appeared above the parapet. Now they are taller and older, and on Coronation Day all hope to see them there again, with their Majesties, a picture of colour and brightness against the grey stone—a picture of a happy and loved Royal Family.

CHAPTER FIVE

THE DEMOCRATIC KING

A SPEAKER said lately on the wireless that the Boys' camp founded by the King when Duke of York was "truly democratic." He might have said the same about the King himself, for our new monarch is a real democrat in the sense that one of the factory boys at that same camp meant when he remarked: "He's really a human being—just one of us."

From the time when he was still a boy, King George has steadily and patiently learnt everything possible about the conditions of the working people all over this Empire: during his year at Cambridge that is what he studied—political economy and social subjects. It is only natural that he should have been called the "Industrial Prince," or "Ambassador of Industry"; he knows more about Factory Acts and wages than many heads of great firms, and has a thorough and practical understanding of the machines which the men and women work.

The King became President of the Industrial Welfare Society when it was founded just after the war, and his duties have taken him to factories, mills, mines and quarries all over the country. Employers and workmen know that it is no use trying to hide things from King George! He has an eagle eye and a habit of making surprise visits in order to see for himself.

At one time he was inspecting a glue-factory, some of the processes in which are so unpleasant and evil-smelling that his companions were anxious that the King should not go into these particular departments. "Why not?" he asked quickly. "People work there, don't they? What's good enough for them is good enough for me."

Another time, a visit had been arranged to a model village, and some of the cottage homes prepared especially for his inspection—which the King guessed at once. Accordingly he contrived to turn aside and knocked, himself, at the door of a little house, where he was *not* expected, and where the wife was just starting her weekly wash. When she opened the door, she stared in utter bewilderment as the King smiled and asked if he might come in.

"I'm so excited I don't know what I'm doing or saying," she answered, but recovered enough to show the royal visitor round her home, which was very clean, in spite of a little untidiness.

Again and again the King has shown this determination to get at the depths of things—even if that thing happens to be a coal-mine, for he has gone underground several times to see the conditions of working. The first time he did this, putting on overalls and a miner's cap and lamp, he insisted on taking a pick and hewing a lump of coal in one of the workings. The shift at the surface meantime had called their brass band together and were waiting at the pithead to greet the Duke of York as he then was. But a figure appeared so covered with coal dust from head to foot as to be unrecognisable—until saluted with the National Anthem, after which the whole crowd broke into: "For he's a jolly good fellow."

The Royalty-hewn lump of coal, by the way, was broken up into tiny pieces as souvenirs, and one of these will be found in every miner's cottage in the neighbourhood of the pit.

Not only the King, but the Queen, too, knows something of what a miner's life must mean, day in, day out, for she accompanied her husband down a pit in Durham, wearing a shawl tied over her head and a waterproof overall.

The King started his public life with the wish, as he said himself, to "Cement that fellowship in all walks of industry which is the backbone of our Imperial progress." What that really means is to put oneself into other folks' shoes—and in that he certainly succeeds.

His democratic ways delighted the people in the Antipodes: New Zealanders are never tired of telling how once when an important deputation was to meet the Royal train at a certain station, the officials assembled on that spot in the platform opposite to which the State carriage would draw up. But the carriage was empty—and when the reception committee looked round, quite bewildered, they saw the grime-streaked face of a youthful figure in blue dungarees thrust through the window of the "cab," a greasy blackened hand waving a lump of tow.

PLATE XVII

ROYAL SILVER JUBILEE PROCESSION: THE ROYAL PARTY PASSING TEMPLE BAR.

A LITTLE WELSH GIRL PRESENTING HIS MAJESTY WITH A CASE OF PIPES, AT GOLF MATCH
IN SOUTH WALES.

PLATE XVIII

PRINCESS ELIZABETH AND HER WELSH COTTAGE, IN THE GROUNDS OF ROYAL LODGE, WINDSOR.

The Duke of York had been enjoying once again the experience of acting amateur engine-driver.

That his sympathy with workers is very real was shown in 1921 when he cancelled a long-standing engagement to attend the Cutlers' Banquet at Sheffield, because, as he said, it would not be right for him to be present at a splendid dinner "while so many workless people were compelled to go hungry."

But while the King's thought and understanding goes out to every worker amongst his subjects, it is to the young people, and especially to work for boys, that he has devoted himself, beginning with his first venture, directly after the war, the Boys' Welfare Society.

It was through this that he learnt so much about the needs and troubles of boys in industry: not content with this, he visited their homes and started schemes to give them more fresh air and exercise by providing playing fields, wherever possible, and by encouraging village settlements to relieve the terrible over-crowding in cities. This was why the King was so keenly interested in the Fairbridge Farm Schools, in Western Australia, that plan made by another young man, the South African Kingsley Fairbridge; to take slum children and give them a new outdoor life overseas. He has never forgotten the happy, healthy children at the Fairbridge schools, near Perth: he said at the time that it was his ideal training for the boys and girls of the Empire.

But since it is impossible to transplant all town-bred boys to the Colonies, the King, who is full of common sense as well as of dreams, just goes on doing everything he can to improve things as they are, until it is possible to make them what they might be. It runs to a long list—those associations of which he is President or Chairman, which aim at bettering conditions for the young. Besides the Boys' Welfare Society, there is the Playing Fields Association, which, of course, aims at giving boys and girls safe recreation places—those children who other-wise would have nowhere to play except the perilous streets.

The King has worked tremendously hard at this scheme, and the way in which his personal interest is appreciated is shown by a nice story which he tells himself. Two small boys called at 145 Piccadilly and explained that their cricket pitch in a certain public park had been taken away from them by the local authorities—and, please, what was the Duke going to do about it? The Duke did not fail them; he made enquiries at once, found that they were quite entitled to use the pitch, tackled those in authority, and not only saw that the ground was put in order, but sent the boys several dozen tennis balls with which to play.

Then the King is patron of the National Safety First Association, one branch of which gives prizes in schools for the best essays on Road Safety and how to take care. As a sign of his active wish to help, King George took part himself in a "Safety First" Film, which was exhibited at many schools and other places.

Perhaps nearest of all to the King's heart is that piece of work which he planned and started entirely after his own ideas—The Duke of York's Camp. And it all began with a football match at which he was asked to referee.

A welfare worker in a factory brought his team of lads up to London to play against Westminster School in their field in Vincent Square. Watching the game, seeing in how friendly a way the Public Schoolboys and factory hands played and talked together, King George wondered what could be done to continue such a happy state of affairs. He hit upon a plan, and proceeded to carry it out, the first "Duke of York's Camp" being held at New Romney in 1921.

Two boys from each of a hundred factories, two more from each of a hundred schools—these have been invited every year since then to the Camp as the Duke's guests. There, twenty "messes" of twenty boys each, half being from Public schools and half working lads, sleep in tents or old army huts, do all the camp jobs together, cook their own meals, each section under a leader, and competing amongst themselves in a very friendly rivalry at all kinds of sports and games. Prizes are given to the winning sections—not to individuals; and there is a "wooden spoon" prize which travels almost yearly from one mess to another and which arose from the chance of the Duke's sharp eye noticing an old packing-case, stencilled: "20 Prime Young Rabbits."

From henceforth the "rabbits" of the twenty sections hold that case and are in honour bound to use it in camp as a seat or table.

After the first season the camp has generally been held at Southwold, and during those fifteen years some six thousand boys have spent a happy and healthy week there and learnt a lesson in real democracy which they are never likely to forget. Another camp for the northern districts has now been started at Chatsworth, but it is to Southwold that the King has gone himself for a couple of days, year after year, only missing one season when he had a badly poisoned hand.

And he goes not as a patron or onlooker, but to be one of his boys, to sing with them round the camp fire, to play, swim, play practical jokes and eat with them, to say—as he was heard to once, on leaving: "I *did* enjoy myself: that's what I call a real holiday." The King's hut—just the same as any of the others except for the words: "Great Chief" inscribed by the boys above the door—is a centre, for the time being, of the camp life. He is up as early as the rest, dashing down to the sea, with a towel round his shoulders, for a cold bathe—so cold that the member of his household who accompanies him often protests, only to be told heartlessly by his master: "Just look what an appetite for breakfast it will give you!"

There are no half measures, either, in his sharing of the games. Asked on one occasion to referee at a game of push-ball, which some of the camp-leaders thought he might find a trifle over-strenuous: "Referee be blowed!" said the King. "I'm going to *play*." Play he did, heaving and struggling with the rest, and in the thick of the scrum a Rugger "blue" shoving with all his might into the ribs of the young man in front of him, shouted: "Play up, can't you? Push like billy ho!" "I *am* pushing like billy ho!" gasped back the King, who was the owner of the bruised ribs just mentioned.

Yes: there are six thousand and more of his new subjects who do not look upon King George as their sovereign only, but also—and it is how he would wish it to be—as a real friend and companion.

There is hardly any boys' associations in which King George has not interested himself at one time or another. He has presided at Scout Jamborees and given the left-handed shake to scouts from all over the world. In May, 1935, he attended the Jubilee tribute to King George V organised by the Boys'

Continued on page 34.

1. KING GEORGE V.
2. QUEEN MARY.
3. THE PRINCE OF WALES (EX-KING EDWARD VIII).
4. THE PRINCESS ROYAL.
5. THE DUKE OF CONNAUGHT.
6. THE QUEEN OF NORWAY.
7. THE DUKE OF YORK (now KING GEORGE VI).
8. THE DUCHESS OF YORK (now QUEEN ELIZABETH).
9. PRINCESS ELIZABETH.
10. PRINCESS MARGARET.
11. THE DUKE OF GLOUCESTER.
12. THE DUCHESS OF KENT.
13. THE DUKE OF KENT.
14. PRINCESS ALICE, COUNTESS OF ATHLONE.
15. THE EARL OF ATHLONE.
16. PRINCESS VICTORIA.

17. PRINCESS LOUISE (Duchess of Argyll).
18. THE MARQUESS OF CARISBROOKE.
19. MADAME DE OLIVEIRA.
20. THE BRAZILIAN AMBASSADOR (Senhor R. R. de Oliveira).
21. THE MAHARAJAH OF PATIALA.
22. THE MAHARAJAH OF BIKANIR.
23. THE MAHARAJAH OF KASHMIR.
24. COLONEL SIR UMAR HAYAT KHAN.
25. THE MARQUESS OF ANGLESEY.
26. LORD GRANARD.
27. SIR KINGSLEY WOOD (Postmaster-General).
28. LORD CROMER (Lord Chamberlain).
29. MR. W. ORMSBY-GORE (First Commissioner of Works.)

30. LORD LEWISHAM (Lord Gr Chamberlain).
31. THE DUKE OF NORFO (Earl Marshal).
32. THE EARL OF HAREWOOD.
33. MR. WINSTON CHURCHILL.
34. MR. GEORGE LANSBURY.
35. LORD HALIFAX (President the Board of Education).
36. MR. LLOYD GEORGE.
37. SIR BOLTON EYRES-MONSE (First Lord of t Admiralty).
38. LORD CRAIGAVON (Pri Minister of Northe Ireland).
39. MR. WALTER RUNCIM (President of the Board Trade).
40. SIR HILTON YOUNG (Minis of Health).

PLATE XIX

HIS MAJESTY IN PLAY AT A TENNIS TOURNAMENT, 1921.

HIS MAJESTY, WHEN DUKE OF YORK, OPERATING THE APPARATUS OF A FILM PHOTOGRAPHER.

PLATE XX

THE HEART OF TH

"The King shall rejo

THE JUBILEE

The Official Picture of the Thanksgiving Service at St. Pa

PLATE XXI

MPIRE, MAY 6TH, 1935

THY strength, O Lord."

Painted by Mr. Frank O. Salisbury, for their Majesties King George V and Queen Mary.   Reproduced by courtesy of "The Times."

GEORGE V.

hedral.   Exhibited at the Royal Academy, 1936.

PLATE XXII

[From the picture by Frank Beresford ; Exhibited Royal Academy, 1936.

"THE PRINCES' VIGIL." 12.15 A.M. JANUARY 28TH, 1936.

His Majesty the King, the Ex-King Edward VIII, the Duke of Gloucester, the Duke of Kent, at the Lying-in-State of King George V.

1. Mr. G. Martin Huggins (Prime Minister of Southern Rhodesia).
2. Sir Joseph Bhore (representing British India).
3. Lord Londonderry (Secretary of State for Air).
4. General Hertzog (Prime Minister of South Africa).
5. Lord Hailsham (Secretary of State for War).
6. Mr. G. W. Forbes (Prime Minister of New Zealand).
7. Sir Philip Cunliffe-Lister (Secretary of State for the Colonies).
8. Mr. J. A. Lyons (Prime Minister of Australia).
0. Mr. R. B. Bennett (Prime Minister of Canada).

51. Sir John Simon (Secretary of State for Foreign Affairs).
52. Mr. Ramsay MacDonald (Prime Minister).
53. Sir John Gilmour (Home Secretary).
54. Captain E. A. FitzRoy (Speaker of the House of Commons).
55. Mr. Neville Chamberlain (Chancellor of the Exchequer).
56. Lord Sankey (Lord Chancellor).
57. Lord Atkin (Lord of Appeal in Ordinary).
58. Mr. Stanley Baldwin (Lord President of the Council).
59. Mrs. Stanley Baldwin.
60. Lord Hanworth (Master of the Rolls).

61. Lord Blanesburgh (Lord of Appeal).
62. Sir Claud Schuster.
64. Lord Hewart (Lord Chief Justice).
65. Sir Sidney Rowlatt.
66. Canon Carnegie.
67. Sir Lancelot Sanderson.
68. Sir Colin Keppel (Serjeant-at-Arms).
69. The Archbishop of Canterbury.
70. Canon Mozley.
71. The Bishop of London.
72. Canon Alexander.
73. Canon H. R. L. Sheppard.
74. The Archdeacon of London (the Ven. E. N. Sharpe).
75. The Dean of St. Paul's (the Very Rev. W. R. Matthews).

Brigade at the Albert Hall, and received on the platform there the silver baton handed to him by the last runner in the great relay race. Three thousand boys, running relays, took part in this, and ran day and night for over 2,300 miles in all. The King is also chairman of the council formed to administer the King George V's Jubilee Trust, which, of course, was raised especially to do good to the young in the distressed areas by building gymnasiums, clubs, workshops and working in all kinds of other ways.

The King carries his work for boys still further—for he is interested in their future, he wants to feel that when they grow up there will be work for all of them, that the terrible drag of unemployment will be lifted at last and the wheel of prosperity freed to move forward. He, together with the Queen, has visited the distressed areas, trying to find some way to solve the problem, or to make the heavy burden lighter. He has studied the difficulties of the cotton industry in Lancashire, visited the Potteries and the Collieries of the Black Country—and realises, through his knowledge of factories and trade conditions, that nothing will really help unemployment so well as a general increase of prosperity.

That is what King George is trying to bring about by every means in his power: that is why, in 1925, he took over the Presidency of the second Wembley Exhibition, although he was then unaccustomed to public speaking, and very shy at attempting it. But he was determined to do all he could to make the Exhibition a success, and for this he worked unceasingly and went through the final ordeal of the opening ceremony in the presence of his father.

In the end that ordeal had its funny side, for an incident took place which must have appealed to the King's sense of humour. It was necessary in the huge space of the Wembley Stadium that the voices of the speakers should be amplified through microphones and the King came to rehearse his speech in this way the day before the opening of the Exhibition. But when he took his place on the platform and began to speak— not a sound was to be heard: the necessary switches had not been turned on.

The King turned to tell the officials of this default when suddenly a huge roaring voice filled the arena—his own, which had been taken in charge by the microphone without his being aware of it, announcing:

"The confounded things aren't working at all!"

One thing is certain: whenever a leader is needed in any movement to help the working classes, to bring prosperity to his Empire, our King will be ready. And we all know that he possesses the three great qualities which he said himself make up leadership—personality, sympathy and, above all idealism.

CHAPTER SIX

THE KING AS A SPORTSMAN

SCHOOLBOY, Sailor, Skyman, Soldier, Sovereign—our King has been all these in turn, but a sportsman all the time, and there is hardly a game or a sport about which he does not know something.

Riding he learnt at a very early age; skating and swimming, too, on the lake at Sandringham: a youthful photograph shows a small Prince Albert diving in the bathing-pool at the London Bath Club. He looks very well on horseback, and plays a good game of polo, as well as hunting whenever he gets a chance—although he gave up his hunting stable during the Industrial crisis, when the Royal Family set an example in economy.

The King was taught shooting and fishing in small boyhood by those best teachers of all—the keepers and ghillies at Sandringham and Balmoral. He shoots in the same way as his father, and nearly as well, which is saying a great deal: for many years, as Duke of York, he took charge of the covers at Sandringham and made all the arrangements for King George's "shoots."

The King is a keen fisherman, a taste which the Queen shares, and their best sport in this way was during their world tour. This recalls a nice story: when fourteen years old, the future King George having whooping-cough, was sent to recover at Loch Muisk, near Balmoral, in charge of an Osborne master, Mr. Watt, a fine fly-fisher, who taught his pupil the art. That pupil, in New Zealand, heard that Mr. Watt was visiting relatives there, and although terribly pressed for time, he spent several hours of his rare leisure in motoring many miles to see his old tutor.

The King and Queen had just spent some days on the coast and at Lake Taupo, where the Queen caught a seven pound trout. The King was determined on something even bigger, and succeeded in capturing a ground shark, or black marlin, weighing more than one hundred and twenty pounds, in the Bay of Islands. When fighting with this big fish, a launchful of Press photographers came so close that the monster nearly escaped under

36

PLATE XXIII

KING GEORGE VI (WHEN DUKE OF YORK) ATTENDING ARMISTICE DAY CEREMONY AT THE CENOTAPH, WHITEHALL, NOVEMBER 11TH, 1936.

Plate XXIV

His Majesty at His Boys' Camp at Southwold.

In Camp at Southwold, Suffolk: a Friendly Chat.

the vessel's keel—on which, as an ear-witness tells us, King George addressed them in "simple, sailorly language."

Another sporting experience on this tour was on the return voyage at Great Hanish Island, in the Red Sea, a black, bare volcanic rock and one of the hottest places in the world. The King insisted on landing from *Renown* at this uninviting spot to stalk a rare kind of gazelle which has the bad taste to live there. The ground was almost red-hot, the heat overwhelming, but the King persevered and secured a head.

Cricket and football were King George's earliest favourites amongst games, but, except at his Boys' Camp, he has not played them much in late years, although he takes a keen interest in the "Tests" and also in Rugger, and is often asked to kick-off at matches. Here he shows both knowledge of the game and a thoughtfulness which boys will appreciate in often starting the game with a "pass." He knows quite well what an advantage a kick down the field might give to the opposite team.

The King is a great believer in squash rackets, played hard and constantly, as a means to keep fit, and at Cambridge always had an hour of fast practice daily. He kept this up during the voyage on *Renown*: in fact, he instituted a whole series of deck games which were very popular on board, although some found them rather *too* strenuous.

A wooden "squash" court had been erected amidships, only about twenty feet square, and with no ventilators to speak of. Yet in spite of its heat, the King played there for some hours daily, as an alternative to deck hockey, which his shipmates preferred, since it took place in the open air. This game was vigorous, but rather lacked rules: it consisted in striking a rope ball or "grummet" all over the deck with walking-sticks, a goal being scored if the "grummet" was knocked overboard.

There was also deck-cricket and deck-tennis, not only the usual game of that name, played by throwing a rope quoit from hand to hand over a net, but another form of the King's own invention in which ordinary rackets and balls were used, struck against a wooden framework with special rules and penalties.

This brings us to the land game which is really the King's favourite—lawn tennis. He is a left-handed player, and a very good one, so good as to be up to the high standard needed to compete in the Wimbledon Championships, a thing which no British Royalty has ever done before.

The King's first success at lawn tennis was when he won the Mixed Doubles at a big competition at Highgate in 1919 with Miss Peggy Bouverie, now Mrs. Ingram. In 1920 he and Wing Commander (now Sir Louis) Greig were doubles' champions for the Royal Air Force—which encouraged them to enter for the Men's Doubles at Wimbledon in 1926.

An incident happened then which shows another side of the King's sportsmanship. The Wimbledon Committee—rather naturally—wanted to "feature" this Royal entry, to arrange for him and his partner to play in the famous Centre Court, where only great stars appear. But King George would allow nothing of the kind; time enough to play in the Centre Court if he reached it by right, he said, otherwise they must take their place as an ordinary pair: so this was what happened, although the partners naturally attracted a great deal of notice. Unluckily they were drawn against the best couple in the Doubles, Roper Barrett and A. W. Gore, who were both former champions, and King George and his partner could not fight their way past the first round. But many who saw the match, including two great women players, Suzanne Lenglen and Lili Alvarez, considered that our King had the makings of a really fine player, given the tremendous practice which a would-be champion needs. He was very steady, said Mademoiselle Lenglen, and never knew when he was beaten.

Since then the King has played all over the world, from A to Z, or rather Australia to Zanzibar: in Uganda the tennis court was the queerest in his experience perhaps, for it was so laid out that the centre line was exactly over the Equator! Whenever the players changed over, they were obliged to "Cross the Line" although not with the usual ceremonies. Later, in Australia, tired as he was after a long day of receptions at Melbourne, he insisted on going to the Lawn Tennis club in the evening, so as to have the pleasure of playing a few sets with the great Champion from "down under," Norman Brookes.

Golf rivals tennis of late years in the King's affections; the fact that his handicap is in the near neighbourhood of ten shows that he is a really good player, and his love for the game dates back to days when he was coached on several courses and possessed a small set of clubs, made for him especially. For a long time when grown up, he played rarely, and said that he much preferred watching good professionals to going round himself. But when he really *did* take it up again, he improved rapidly and was soon playing a very strong game.

He showed this when opening a new course at Richmond: in spite of a large and noisy audience and to their great delight, King George drove off with a splendid swing, sending his ball considerably more than two hundred yards down the fairway. When made Captain of the "Royal and Ancient" at St. Andrews, too, he distinguished himself by a very good drive, which speaks well for his nerve.

The King is a thoroughly good-tempered golfer. On a certain occasion he travelled all the way down to the West to play against Mr. Frank Hodges, M.P., on a Welsh course. Almost at the last green a dog darted out of the crowd and entirely spoilt what should have been a winning putt for the King, thus losing the hole and the game. Most players show some irritation at such an incident, but the King took it as a joke. It is not surprising that he is very popular amongst caddies on any course where he plays: a red-headed lad whom he often chose at Sunningdale was much envied amongst his fellows for the honour.

Since he left the Flying Force—although fully qualified as a pilot—the King has not shown any particular leaning towards using the air-road, nor did he, as Duke of York, possess 'planes of his own. As a matter of fact he was always keener on the mechanical side of aviation than the actual flying, although he uses it fairly often when rapid travel is necessary. He flew to London, for instance, with his brother, immediately after King George V's death. Motoring really appeals to him more, and he is an excellent driver, with a decided liking for speed, which he showed on one occasion in New Zealand. When he was motoring in that country, the police always provided a car to go some two hundred yards ahead of the Royal vehicle, as a safeguard. The King, being anxious to make a surprise visit to a certain settlement, without wasting time, waited till they were beyond the town boundaries and then told the chauffeur to put on speed. In a few seconds they passed the police car like greased lightning and went speeding on towards their destination, whilst the constables returned to report the matter to their inspector. He was exceedingly angry at this failure in duty and demanded why they had not gone faster to pass the Royal car. "Well, we *were* going at about fifty miles an hour at the time," the sergeant answered. "But *he* went faster." When King George returned to the town, after having seen all he wanted, he apologised for giving his escort the slip, adding with a smile: "But I did make sure that the road was clear! And you mustn't blame the constables—they couldn't stop me."

After that, it is easily understood why the King was described in the Antipodes as a "honest-to-goodness sportsman." It is just the character which he has earned all over his Empire.

CHAPTER SEVEN

THE QUEEN AND HER CHILDREN

ON August 4th, 1900, was born a little girl, whose pet name as though prophetically, was "Princess Elizabeth." The birthplace of Lady Elizabeth Angela Marguerite Bowes-Lyon was St. Paul's, Waldenbury, the beautiful Hertfordshire home of her parents, the Earl and Countess of Strathmore, a warmly-red Tudor house surrounded by the woodland gardens which were to be the setting of an important scene in Lady Elizabeth's life.

Although born in England, most of the future Queen's childhood was spent at her Scottish home, Glamis Castle. And Glamis, grey, ancient and haunted, with its history and legends, is a true home for a fairy-tale Princess, with that arresting beauty of colouring which comes from black hair, blue eyes and the complexion of a wild-rose. Like that same fairy Princess, too, she had the "happy-ever-after" disposition: all who knew her say that there never was a sweeter-tempered baby and child, always smiling, unless someone she had loved looked sad, when small Lady Elizabeth was full of sympathy. One of her early sayings is too charming not to repeat: someone speaking of a very rich man, said it was such a pity he was sure to be only married for his money. The little girl, overhearing, frowned thoughtfully. "But someone *might* do it 'cos they loved him," she murmured.

The Queen would probably say that no child could have been unhappy at Glamis and Waldenbury, in such surroundings and with such a family. She and her brother, David, were very near together in age and as devoted as any twins: they made a charming couple as tiny children in picturesque costumes. Later, and very full of mischief, one of their favourite games at Glamis was to "play ghosts," dressing up to represent one of the many spirits who are supposed to haunt the old castle.

Very early, Lady Elizabeth showed that devotion for her many pets which her own small daughters inherit: the greatest grief of her childhood was the death of a bull-finch, Bobby; very early she made her first appearance in public, an adorable baby bridesmaid at the wedding of her brother, the Master of Glamis: very early, she showed traces of the future perfect hostess, when she entertained her mother's visitors—Lady Strathmore being out—pouring out their tea from a silver pot almost as large as herself.

The atmosphere of Glamis Castle, so soaked in Scottish history, with "Duncan's Room," "Prince Charlie's Room," and "Sir Walter's Room," the heather- and pine-covered hills around would have made an English girl Highland-hearted, and Lady Elizabeth was descended from Scottish Kings. She knows the legends, the lore, the songs of that land of hers—she who is the first Queen from North Britain since Matilda of Scotland so many centuries ago.

During the Christmas season, when Lady Elizabeth was barely five, she met a shy, ten-year-old schoolboy at a children's party. Far from shy herself, she smiled at him over an outsized slice of iced cake—and the boy Prince Albert never quite forgot his first meeting with that smiling child.

Lady Elizabeth was exactly fourteen on that August day when war began, old enough to realise and remember the sadness of it all, to feel the loss of her brother, Lord Fergus, who was killed in France in 1915. Before this happened, Glamis Castle had been turned into a war hospital, and instead of going to school abroad as was planned, Lady Elizabeth began to take her share in looking after the wounded soldiers who came to Glamis. She said that her first war work was crumpling up tissue-paper to make it so soft that it would not crackle in sleeping-bags!

When the soldiers at Glamis heard of the death of Lord Fergus, they were so anxious to show their sympathy, that, quite without being asked, they stopped all singing and gramophone-playing in the wards. It was only when Lady Strathmore noticed the silence and made enquiries that they were persuaded to amuse themselves again.

During the war, when Lady Elizabeth was about sixteen, an exciting thing happened at Glamis, which gave her the chance to show great bravery and coolness. One day, most of the wounded had been sent to a cinema in the nearest town and there were few people in the castle when Lady Elizabeth noticed smoke and sparks and knew that her home was on fire. Without wasting a moment, she ran to the telephone and summoned not only the local brigade, but that from Dundee, then told those members of the family and servants who were in the house.

But the fire was spreading fast and the keep of Glamis Castle is nearly ninety feet high—so high that the fire-hose of the local brigade were not long enough to carry water pumped up from the river Dean so far. The smoke thickened and sparks set fire to the roof in several places: it seemed as though the wonderful old castle, with all the treasures it held, *must* be burnt to the ground —and it certainly would have been if Lady Elizabeth had not sent that call to the Dundee Brigade.

Meanwhile another danger threatened the castle—and again it was Lady Elizabeth who did the right thing. A huge lead tank on the roof, used for storing water, burst with the heat and a cataract poured down the great stone staircase and would have poured through all the rooms too, if she had not called for volunteers to divert the flood with brooms, so that it rushed harmlessly down into the basement. Then she formed a chain of twenty or thirty people between the chief rooms and the front door to pass along from hand to hand into safety the most valuable pictures, china and other treasures. While they were doing this with the fire still gaining, the Dundee Brigade dashed up and after a fierce fight the Castle was really saved.

It was not until the end of 1919 that the last wounded men left Glamis, and not long after this Lady Elizabeth and Prince Albert met again. Another three years passed before their engagement was announced, and it is said that the Prince proposed several times. If so, the truth is more likely what one of her friends said afterwards—that "Elizabeth did not really want to marry the King's son, but found that she could not live without Bertie."

However that may be, there came a certain Saturday, January 13th, 1923—a lucky 13th!—when the Duke came down for the week-end to Waldenbury, and on the Sunday morning persuaded Lady Elizabeth to go for a walk with him in the wooded garden. After that—well, as Lady Elizabeth said herself when writing to tell a friend of her great happiness, "the cat is out of the bag, and there is no chance of stuffing it back again."

We know already many of the things which happened after that, at home and abroad. Now it is time to see something more of the King and Queen's daughters, Elizabeth Alexandra Mary, born on April 21st, 1926, and Margaret Rose, whose birthday was August 21st, 1930.

Both the Princesses were christened in the private chapel at Buckingham Palace by the Archbishop of Canterbury, both wearing the same lace robe which four generations of Royal babies have worn, and were christened in Jordan water from the small golden "Lily" font which was made in 1840 for the christening of all Queen Victoria's children. At both the christenings, too, there was a big white cake, with a baby doll in a silver cradle on the top.

Whilst her parents were abroad and Princess Elizabeth lived mostly at Buckingham Palace, she became a great favourite with Londoners, who loved to see the baby drive out with her nurse, often dressed in a yellow bonnet and frilly frock which made her look just like a golden buttercup. Passing the sentries at the Palace gates, she would gravely return their salutes with a tiny hand in its fingerless glove, and it is said that the small Princess missed the soldiers on guard when she went to her other grandparents at Glamis and asked in quite offended tones: "Where are my sentries?"

After her father and mother came home with all those wonderful presents of toys and pets from the other side of the world, the little family went to live at 145 Piccadilly, and Princess Elizabeth was established in the delightful nurseries with barred windows, cherry-red carpets and a big Sheraton glass-fronted bookcase for a toy cupboard, where a few years later the new tiny sister joined her.

When Princess Elizabeth was two years old, her mother became Colonel of a Regiment, and a "White Rose" Regiment, too, the King's Own Yorkshire Light Infantry, known always as the "Koylis." At about the same time she went to an entertainment which her small daughter would have much enjoyed a few years later. This was a Dolls' Parade, in aid of the Princess Elizabeth Hostel, and everybody was supposed to take a doll dressed exactly like themselves. But the lifesize doll carried by the Duchess of York was a very good copy of the real Princess Elizabeth.

To return to the nursery at "145," Princess Elizabeth has a special Swiss chair there of coloured wood carved with chamois: when sat in, the sounds of an "Alphorn" playing a tune are heard. In the night nursery rosebuds are painted on the white beds, with

PLATE XXV

THEIR MAJESTIES ARRIVING WITH THEIR CHILDREN TO PRESENT COLOURS TO THE 4TH AND 5TH BLACK WATCH, AT GLAMIS, 1935.

THEIR MAJESTIES AND THE PRINCESSES AT THE ROYAL MILITARY TOURNAMENT, 1936.

PLATE XXVI

HIS MAJESTY DRIVING A TRAM THROUGH THE STREETS OF GLASGOW, AFTER OPENING THE
NEW RECREATION GROUND, 1924.

HIS MAJESTY INSPECTING THE MINIATURE RAILWAY AT NEW ROMNEY, KENT, 1926.

pink brushes and combs. Each Princess has her own china at meals—Elizabeth's with a pair of magpies and the motto "Two for Joy" on blue and white, while Margaret Rose's china is pink and white with love-birds on a heather-spray.

Princess Margaret Rose still likes play-time and toys best, but Princess Elizabeth is very fond of her lessons, and especially of history, and of being taken to see the places where things happened and famous people lived. She has a scrapbook, too, into which she sticks the photographs of Royal children, copying out anything which she reads about them and tracing their relationship to herself and her sister. In fact, Princess Elizabeth is very like her father in wanting to know and get to the bottom of things: she is like him, too, in her enjoyment of understanding radio sets and mechanical or electric toys of any kind.

That is one reason why she and Princess Margaret Rose were so interested in their visit to Beconscot, that fascinating model village built in his own garden at Beaconsfield by an amateur engineer. It is the most wonderful place imaginable, just like a real village seen through the wrong end of a telescope, with a railway station, with real minute trains, a street with a church and shops, public gardens with dwarf-trees and flowers and even a sea-port with ships and an air-port with aeroplanes.

Princess Elizabeth has ridden since she was a tiny child of three, first on an equally tiny pony given to her by her grandfather, King George, now on her father's present, a bay horse, which arrived last birthday. None of her photographs are nicer than those which show the Princess in riding-coat and *jodhpur* breeches, and probably soon Princess Margaret Rose will join her on horseback. Already both have bicycles, which they love, and the elder Princess is quite a trick cyclist, riding without touching the handlebars and performing various other feats. Both are being taught to swim, and last summer Princess Elizabeth could already take six or seven strokes without touching the bottom.

Another outdoor occupation which has become a great favourite of late is gardening—for Princess Elizabeth, at Royal Lodge, Windsor, has her own garden, surrounding her own house, with lawns, sundial and flower-beds all complete.

This brings us to that possession which most girls will envy Princess Elizabeth more than anything else, the little thatched

house of her very own, "Y Bwthyn Bach"—"Small House"—
which was given to her by the people of Wales some years ago.
An adventurous house, too, for it travelled to Windsor all the
way from Wales by road on a big lorry. Worse than that, before
it had got half way, there was a cry of "Fire!" and the Princesses' cottage was seen to be in flames, like her mother's castle
long before. Luckily the fire was put out before much damage
was done, but the little house had to be sent back to its builders
for repairs, and Princess Elizabeth must have felt very impa-
tient before all was well, the second road journey taken and
the house set up in the middle of the rose garden at Royal
Lodge.

It has two storeys with six rooms, and it is all absolutely and
entirely *real*, with hot and cold water, a bathroom, a wireless
set and electric light. It is completely furnished, kitchen and
all, with everything which the heart of a girl could desire, and
nobody except the two Princesses has any hand in its cleaning
and tidying. They sweep and brush and scrub and beat the rugs:
the red and white check curtains in the windows are washed and
ironed by themselves—although Princess Elizabeth has been
heard to complain that *she* does most of the work and that
Princess Margaret Rose is dreadfully untidy.

So the little house teaches all sorts of lessons in housekeeping
by making play of them: even cooking is one of them, for at the
annual party at Blaina (Mon.) given for the juvenile unemployment instruction centre, there was a fine iced cake with a message
from the Queen:

"This cake was made and iced by Princess Elizabeth before
she left Sandringham."

It is a fine place to entertain the young friends and relations
of the Princesses, although their cousins, Lord Lascelles and
Gerald Lascelles, who were Princess Elizabeth's chief playmates
when younger, are now rather big schoolboys for such games.
But another small family of cousins is growing up to love the
little house—Prince Edward of Kent, the son of their uncle,
the Duke of Kent, the little boy who will soon be two years old
and that latest member of our Royal family, the tiny Princess
who was born on Christmas Day to be a particularly nice present
for her mother, Princess Marina, as well as for the whole Empire
and the children of that Empire above all, who heard of her

birth just when they were receiving their gifts in remembrance of another Child's birthday, the baby Jesus Himself.

It must have been an especially wonderful surprise for Princess Elizabeth and her sister, keeping their Christmas as usual at Sandringham, that happy country home, where the chief event of the day is the monster tree in the afternoon, from which presents are given to all the staff and many of the tenants on the estate. It is almost as though the new Baby Princess had come at Christmas to fill just a little, as only a baby could, the blank left since the Christmas before by the death of King George. Princess Elizabeth especially must have missed her grandfather very much: he and she were always the greatest of friends, and a pretty story is told of one of her earliest Christmasses at Sandringham. She heard the waits singing of "good will to all mankind" and afterwards remarked with her arms round King George's neck: "*I* know that old man kind: it's you, grandpa, and I *do* love you."

"We will have *such* fun together!" Princess Elizabeth said, nearly seven years ago, when she first heard of her new baby sister—and they have gone on having fun ever since, for they are both happy-natured children, like their mother before them and, like her, brought up very simply and in a homely way in spite of their Royal birth. There is a story of a little slum child who said that if she was a Princess, she would have ice-cream and chocolates for every meal, but that is certainly not the diet of our own two real Princesses. Plenty of fruit and bread and butter, not many sweets or rich things seem to be the main idea, and it was quite an event when each in turn was promoted from milk to real—if weak—tea.

It seems likely that both the Princesses will sing well, for they have very sweet voices, and the elder, at least, has always been decidedly musical. A very early present was a miniature piano, on which she learnt scales and simple tunes, but now she is promoted to the big grand, on which the Queen plays.

The pair are not spoilt by going to a great number of entertainments: that is easily seen by the way in which they enjoy everything. At the Royal Tournament, the Aldershot Tattoo, or the Christmas circus at Olympia, no children are so intent on the performance or so keenly interested. Nothing bored about *them!* It is the same when, now, they sometimes go with their mother to sales of work and charity bazaars: everything is examined very seriously, and they make their own selections, Princess Elizabeth paying for the tin of sweets and the woolly ball from her own little handbag with a crowned E, made by disabled soldiers and given to her—with a small chair for the younger Princess—at a sale which they helped the Queen to open.

It has always been said of Queen Elizabeth that when she receives a bouquet at one of these functions, she takes it and gives thanks for it as though she had never been given flowers in her life before, so surprised and delighted she seems. That is the very Royalty of politeness, yet it is not put on, any more than that charming natural smile of hers which the Princesses have inherited. Already they know just how to behave in public, and Princess Elizabeth gave away the prizes to the young competitors at the last Richmond Horse Show in a most graciously royal way.

Fortunately most of their lives are still more or less private: they still play energetic games of their own invention at Windsor or in London. A favourite some months ago was "Traffic Blocks" played in the garden behind "145," Princess Elizabeth exceeding the speed-limit on her bicycle and held up by the raised white-gloved hand of her younger sister, taking the part of a traffic "cop."

More carefree still is their life at Windsor, with their menagerie of pets; fawns, parrots, twenty budgerigars and above all the dogs they all love. There are the family of golden Labradors, who are the King's favourites, Mimsey and her son and daughter, Stiffy and Scrummy. Choo-choo is a hairy-coated animal and much beloved, while the particular pets of the two Princesses are their own Welsh "corgis," Jane and Dookie, who belong to a race of small, devotedly faithful sheepdogs peculiar to Wales.

Even at home the girls are trained to be thoughtful for others. Constantly one sees on the list of garments sent to some charity, scarves knitted by the two Princesses, and every Christmas there is a tremendous overhaul of their toys and big boxes are sent off to Children's Hospitals and Homes—not by any means unwanted toys, either, but real favourites which they would gladly keep themselves, but are ready and willing to send to

PLATE XXVII

THEIR MAJESTIES ABOUT TO DESCEND A COAL MINE IN DURHAM, 1936.

QUEEN MARY AND PRINCESS ELIZABETH VISITING THE MODEL VILLAGE OF BEKONSCOT IN 1934.

PLATE XXVIII

His Majesty in Highland Dress Arriving at St. Giles' Cathedral, Edinburgh.

PLATE XXIX

THEIR MAJESTIES AT EDINBURGH DURING THE JUBILEE CELEBRATIONS OF KING GEORGE V.

THEIR MAJESTIES BEING INTRODUCED TO MEMBERS OF THE COUNCIL AT THE
ROYAL AGRICULTURAL SHOW, SOUTHAMPTON, 1932.

PLATE XXX

HER MAJESTY, AS DUCHESS OF YORK, AT THE NEW PLAYGROUND ON THE SITE OF THE OLD
FOUNDLING HOSPITAL, 1936.

THEIR MAJESTIES ACCOMPANIED BY PRINCESS ELIZABETH AND PRINCESS MARGARET ROSE
ARRIVING AT THE ROYAL MILITARY TOURNAMENT, 1936.

other less lucky boys and girls. They have been taught, too, to take time and trouble mending the breakages in any toys to be sent away, and they carefully wash and iron the clothes of any dolls among the gifts.

Of Queen Elizabeth it was said by one who knows her: "She is so kind: she never forgets those little things which count in making others happy." That same kindness and thoughtfulness she has taught her children; small wonder that she and they are greatly loved by all her husband's subjects.

CHAPTER EIGHT

THE CORONATION

ON May 12th, 1937, when the parks and green places of London are at their best in Spring freshness, a Sovereign of the British nation and his Consort will ride in State to Westminster to be crowned in the Abbey Church of Edward the Confessor, to take part in the most solemn ceremonial of a King or an Emperor's life. For every smallest part of the coronation rites is filled with meaning, leading up to the consecration of the monarch to the service of God and his country.

The ceremony itself carries us back a thousand years and more through the long line of our Sovereigns. In Anglo-Saxon days the kings were "hallowed," to use the old word, seated upon that ancient stone which gives its name of the King's Stone to Kingston-on-Thames, and still stands in the town's market-place.

Now, the coronation chair of oak, resting on four carved lions, made in 1300 by order of King Edward I for one hundred shillings and used by all our monarchs since the crowning of Edward II in 1308, has beneath its seat the no less ancient "Stone of Scone," a rough sandstone block brought to the Abbey from Scotland by King Edward in 1296.

It was the custom amongst our Saxon kings to be reconsecrated by the archbishops and wear their crowns three times every year, at Easter, Whitsun and Christmas, and some religious festival was generally chosen for the actual coronation day. Edward the Confessor was crowned at Easter, William the Conqueror at Christmas, Charles II, James II, and Queen Anne all on St. George's Day. May 12th is the Feast-day of Saint Joan of Arc, whose monument stands in Winchester Cathedral, where several English kings were crowned in old times.

Almost every part of the wonderful coronation ceremony can be traced back to antiquity. For instance, the old chronicle of Geoffrey of Monmouth tells of the "hallowing" of the partly legendary King Arthur, whose stories, with those of his Knights of the Round Table, many of us know. This chronicler describes the four gold swords carried by four lesser kings at Arthur's coronation—and four swords are still carried before our kings; the sword of state, the curtana, or pointless sword of mercy, and the two sharp-pointed swords of temporal and spiritual justice; they play a great part in the ceremony before the actual coronation.

The State sword of offering is double-handled, the scabbard covered with crimson velvet studded with gold plaques bearing the emblems of the three kingdoms. It is carried in the Royal procession by a State official, but later the Archbishop of Canterbury, after laying it on the altar, girds the King with it, aided by the Lord Great Chamberlain, to show that he will defend his people and punish wrongdoers. Then the King himself offers it upon the altar, from which the peer who bears the sword by right "redeems" it for one hundred shillings and carries it naked before the King for the rest of the ceremony. Other peers and officials, who have held the right for generations, carry the three other swords.

In one way, ancient Saxon ceremonies are not continued at the present day, for kings and queens then usually went to their crowning sitting in a cart drawn by white oxen which were afterwards sacrificed. This year, as in the past two centuries, the splendid "glass coach" will be used, which may be seen by visitors to London in the Royal mews at Buckingham Palace with its gilded palm-trees and the shells and tritons which represent Britain's dominions over the seas. This coach, with its painted panels and velvet cushions, is as gorgeous inside as out: it will be drawn at the coronation by a team of the "Windsor Greys," but until the war, the famous Hanoverian cream-coloured ponies were used on State occasions.

Whilst the State Coach drives slowly through the streets, the Abbey itself, hung and carpeted with blue and gold for the ceremony, fills with clergy, high officials, peers and peeresses and the pursuivants and heralds of the College of Arms in their splendid robes and jewels, making the grand old church the most wonderful scene imaginable.

At the West door, the King and Queen are met by the Archbishop of Canterbury, the choir and clergy, with the procession of the regalia, carried by officials whose rights are settled by the Court of Claims. Some of these claims and privileges are very strange, and one of the most curious is that of the King's Bargemaster. In old days, the Thames was the "Royal Road" through London: the palaces of Whitehall, the Tower, Greenwich, Richmond and Hampton Court were all on its banks, so the Sovereign travelled everywhere in the State Barge and his barge-master had charge of the Royal crown itself, the sign of sovereignty. Times have changed: the King and crown no longer travel by water: but the Royal Bargemaster keeps his ancient privilege and still rides in the carriage which brings the crown of England to its destination on State occasions.

Other queer claims deal with such matters as the right to strew herbs before the Sovereign: to sit with head covered in the Royal presence: to serve out the napkins at State banquets and offer salt on these occasions—afterwards taking the salt-cellars as perquisites. The Lord Great Chamberlain has the ancient right to array the King in his state robes for the ceremony: equally old is the claim of the two Bishops of Durham and Bath and Wells to support His Majesty. Formerly, the Lord Great Chamberlain also demanded the bed, with its hangings and covers, on which the Sovereign slept the night before the coronation, together with the other furniture of the room, and forty ells of crimson velvet for his own mantle. But these rights are *not* claimed nowadays.

In the procession, Bishops carry the Bible, paten and chalice; peers and high officers the crowns, swords, the spoon and ampulla (or eagle-shaped gold vessel for anointing) the sceptres, orb, ring and gloves—all ancient symbolical objects called the regalia. The *right-hand* glove, presented by the Lord of the manor of Worksop, now the Duke of Newcastle, carries the privilege of supporting the King's right arm. The great gold spurs, with crimson velvet gold-embroidered straps, are carried by the two descendants of the noble who bore them at the coronation of Richard Coeur de Lion.

Every part of the regalia is beautiful and historic. There are four sceptres, two which the King holds later in his right and left hands and two for the Queen. The Royal sceptre with the cross is of gold, splendidly enamelled and jewelled, its chief gem part of the largest diamond in the world, the Star of Africa. The Sceptre with the Dove, or Rod of Equity, is surmounted by a white enamelled Dove, the Holy Spirit of Wisdom and Justice. The Queen's sceptres are like those of the King, but less heavy.

PLATE XXXI

THEIR MAJESTIES ACCOMPANIED BY THE PRINCESSES AT PERTH, FOR THE OPENING OF THE NEW ART GALLERY.

HIS MAJESTY INSPECTING THE GUARD OF HONOUR OF THE BLACK WATCH AT PERTH IN AUGUST, 1935, WHEN HE AND THE QUEEN (THEN DUKE AND DUCHESS OF YORK) WERE PRESENTED WITH THE FREEDOM OF THE CITY.

Plate XXXII

The "Queen Mary."

[By courtesy of "The Times"

The great Cunard White Star liner under Construction at Clydebank. Launched by H.M. Queen Mary, 1934.

Then there is the orb, a ball of gold, to be held in the King's hand, with a jewelled cross on the top of it.

In the procession of the regalia are also carried the standards of the three kingdoms and the Empire. The great standard of England is carried by the King's Champion, an office held by members of the Dymoke family for many centuries. The Champion had the right to challenge any to single combat who questioned the Sovereign's claim to the throne, riding on "the best horse but one" from the Royal stables. Until the reign of William IV the Dymoke of the day actually did make this challenge at every coronation, riding into Westminster Hall in full armour and throwing down a gauntlet.

The way in which the coronation ceremony grows and has been enlarged, as years go by and the Empire extends, is shown by the fact that the standards of Wales, India and the great Dominions overseas were carried for the first time at the coronation of King George V. The emblems embroidered on them are those of the young new countries, not heraldic signs, but ships, wheat-sheaves, farm-waggons and other symbols of commerce and agriculture.

As the King enters the Abbey, the central figure now in the procession, he wears a crimson satin tunic reaching to his knees, silk breeches and stockings and court shoes. Over this is the crimson velvet imperial mantle, with a cape of the white fur called miniver and on his head the Cap of State, or maintenance, of crimson velvet turned up with ermine.

Now comes the first part of the coronation service called the Recognition, when the King shows himself to be chosen by his people, standing on the gorgeously carpeted platform near the altar, which is called the Theatre. Four times the Archbishop of Canterbury cries loudly, facing in turn the four points of the compass: "Sirs, I here present unto you George, the undoubted King of this realm: wherefore all you who are come this day to do your homage and service, are you willing to do the same?"

Four times the thunderous answer comes, a shout of, "God save King George!" followed by a fanfare of trumpets. Each time the shout is begun by fifty scholars from Westminster School, who have had the right to lead these cheers for many centuries in their own fashion. "Vivat Regina Elizabetha!"—the boys shout. "Vivat Rex Georgius!"

The splendid service goes on: the regalia is laid upon the altar and the King, preceded by the sword of state, goes bareheaded to lay his hand upon the Bible and take the coronation oath, solemnly promising to govern the realm according to law and custom.

Then he seats himself in the King Edward's chair upon the ancient stone for the "hallowing" or anointing with oil. During this "sacring," four Knights of the Garter hold a cloth-of-gold canopy over the monarch. Next comes the robing and investiture, each part of the dress and regalia having its own meaning. The long white cambric tunic or alb, the short super-tunica of cloth-of-gold show that he is a priest as well as temporal sovereign to his people: the gold girdle, given by the Worshipful Company of Girdlers is fastened about him, the armill laid across his shoulders, a scarf or stole embroidered with the emblems of the Dominions, the Southern Cross for Australia, the lotus for India the mimosa for South Africa. Over all is the pallium, or robe royal, a long cloak of cloth-of-gold interwoven with flowers of the most gorgeous colours.

The orb is placed for a moment in the monarch's hand, then returned to the altar while he is reminded that "the whole world is subject to the Empire of Christ." Then the ring which unites the King to his people is placed by the Archbishop upon His Majesty's fourth finger—the wedding finger of the times before 1549. It is pure gold, set with a ruby on which a cross is engraved. This ring is newly-made at each coronation, and tradition says, the more closely it fits, the longer will the reign last. This was certainly true in Queen Victoria's case, for she tells us the ring was so tight that it had to be forced on and hurt terribly when it was removed.

The two sceptres are placed in the King's hands—and now the greatest moment comes. The Archbishop holds up St. Edward's Crown, pearls, diamonds, emeralds, rubies and sapphires covering the four crosses and four fleur-de-lys, the surmounting cross set with three pearls. And as the gleaming crown slowly descends upon the King's head, there comes a sudden blaze of light, a wave of glittering colour as all the peers put on their coronets. The tense, breathless silence breaks, as the Abbey bells crash out, the Tower guns thunder, trumpets peal and drums beat a point of war, amidst shouts from all in the Abbey of: "Long live the King!"

As the crown is placed on the King's head, the Archbishop pronounces the beautiful prayer: "Be strong and play the man! Keep the commandments of the Lord thy God and walk in His ways all the days of your life."

The crowning of the Queen then takes place, with much the same rites, the actual ceremony being usually performed by the Archbishop of York, when all the peeresses place their coronets upon their own heads at the moment of Her Majesty's crowning. Then, robed and wearing crown and regalia, the monarch returns to the Chair of State upon the Theatre, is "lifted up into it" by the spiritual and temporal peers, to quote the curious words of the service-book, interesting because they refer to the old days when newly-crowned kings actually *were* "lifted" upon the shields and shoulders of their nobles.

Now comes the homage, the first to pay it being the Archbishop of Canterbury, afterwards the Princes of the Blood, and peers according to their rank, swearing to become His Majesty's liege men "of life and limb and earthly worship": to "bear faith and truth, to live and die against all manner of folks." Shouts, trumpets, beating of drums ends this ceremony—the people's homage.

The Sovereign then lays down the sceptres, removes the crown, and kneels with his Consort before the altar to take the Sacrament and to present the traditional offering "a pall or altar-cloth and an ingot or wedge of gold of a pound weight."

There the wonderful rites uniting Sovereign and Empire end in the Abbey which will have seen the coronation of forty monarchs. After disrobing in St. Edward's Chapel, the King, with the Queen, enters the State Coach again at the West door to drive to Buckingham Palace, amid cheering crowds and crashing bells. In one of the State carriages which follow will sit the most interesting figures in the ceremony next to their Majesties, Princess Elizabeth, the heiress presumptive and Princess Margaret Rose, her sister, wearing—at least so it is expected and hoped —the furred velvet mantles and coronets of their rank.

Riding home amongst their people the King and Queen still wear Royal robes, crimson velvet and ermine cloaks. The King carries sceptre and orb and wears now the Imperial State Crown. This, unlike the other, used only at the coronation, is worn on State occasions, and is set with many famous jewels,

among them the great ruby, worn by Edward the Black Prince
in his helmet, and afterwards by King Henry V at Agincourt,
a sapphire which was found in Edward the Confessor's tomb
and the huge pearls which were Queen Elizabeth's ear-rings.
This crown, originally made for Queen Victoria, has been
enlarged and enriched for her successors, and in the centre of the
circlet of alternate diamonds, emeralds and sapphires is set the
huge "Star of South Africa" diamond.

The Queen's Imperial Crown is all of diamonds, large and
small, very light and fairylike. But the loveliest gem is the most
famous diamond in the world, the Koh-i-Noor, or Mountain of
Light, given to Queen Victoria when she became Empress of
India and—as an ancient legend says—lucky to every woman who
wears it.

So ends the greatest day in the lives of any sovereigns, for themselves and their people. Above all, this is true in the case of
our Empire, where the crown's circle in a very real sense binds
together the far-flung Dominions of the British Commonwealth
of Nations to that small mother island: "This precious stone set
in a silver sea"—"this Sceptre'd Isle . . . this Throne of Kings
. . . this England!"

MADE AND PRINTED IN GREAT BRITAIN BY PURNELL AND SONS, LTD.
PAULTON (SOMERSET) AND LONDON